Lecture Notes in Economics and Mathematical Systems

For information about Vols. 1–156, please contact your bookseller or Springer-Verlag

Vol. 157: Optimization and Operations Research. Proceedings 1977. Edited by R. Henn, B. Korte, and W. Oettli. VI, 270 pages. 1978.

Vol. 158: L. J. Cherene, Set Valued Dynamical Systems and Economic Flow. VIII, 83 pages. 1978.

Vol. 159: Some Aspects of the Foundations of General Equilibrium Theory: The Posthumous Papers of Peter J. Kalman. Edited by J. Green. VI, 167 pages. 1978.

Vol. 160: Integer Programming and Related Areas. A Classified Bibliography. Edited by D. Hausmann. XIV, 314 pages. 1978.

Vol. 161: M. J. Beckmann, Rank in Organizations. VIII, 164 pages. 1978.

Vol. 162: Recent Developments in Variable Structure Systems, Economics and Biology. Proceedings 1977. Edited by R. R. Mohler and A. Ruberti. VI, 326 pages. 1978.

Vol. 163: G. Fandel, Optimale Entscheidungen in Organisationen. VI, 143 Seiten. 1979.

Vol. 164: C. L. Hwang and A. S. M. Masud, Multiple Objective Decision Making – Methods and Applications. A State-of-the-Art Survey. XII, 351 pages. 1979.

Vol. 165: A. Maravall, Identification in Dynamic Shock-Error Models. VIII, 158 pages. 1979.

Vol. 166: R. Cuninghame-Green, Minimax Algebra. XI, 258 pages. 1979.

Vol. 167: M. Faber, Introduction to Modern Austrian Capital Theory. X, 196 pages. 1979.

Vol. 168: Convex Analysis and Mathematical Economics. Proceedings 1978. Edited by J. Kriens. V, 136 pages. 1979.

Vol. 169: A. Rapoport et al., Coalition Formation by Sophisticated Players. VII, 170 pages. 1979.

Vol. 170: A. E. Roth, Axiomatic Models of Bargaining. V, 121 pages. 1979.

Vol. 171: G. F. Newell, Approximate Behavior of Tandem Queues. XI, 410 pages. 1979.

Vol. 172: K. Neumann and U. Steinhardt, GERT Networks and the Time-Oriented Evaluation of Projects. 268 pages. 1979.

Vol. 173: S. Erlander, Optimal Spatial Interaction and the Gravity Model. VII, 107 pages. 1980.

Vol. 174: Extremal Methods and Systems Analysis. Edited by A. V. Fiacco and K. O. Kortanek. XI, 545 pages. 1980.

Vol. 175: S. K. Srinivasan and R. Subramanian, Probabilistic Analysis of Redundant Systems. VII, 356 pages. 1980.

Vol. 176: R. Färe, Laws of Diminishing Returns. VIII, 97 pages. 1980.

Vol. 177: Multiple Criteria Decision Making-Theory and Application. Proceedings, 1979. Edited by G. Fandel and T. Gal. XVI, 570 pages. 1980.

Vol. 178: M. N. Bhattacharyya, Comparison of Box-Jenkins and Bonn Monetary Model Prediction Performance. VII, 146 pages. 1980.

Vol. 179: Recent Results in Stochastic Programming. Proceedings, 1979. Edited by P. Kall and A. Prékopa. IX, 237 pages. 1980.

Vol. 180: J. F. Brotchie, J. W. Dickey and R. Sharpe, TOPAZ – General Planning Technique and its Applications at the Regional, Urban, and Facility Planning Levels. VII, 356 pages. 1980.

Vol. 181: H. D. Sherali and C. M. Shetty, Optimization with Disjunctive Constraints. VIII, 156 pages. 1980.

Vol. 182: J. Wolters, Stochastic Dynamic Properties of Linear Econometric Models. VIII, 154 pages. 1980.

Vol. 183: K. Schittkowski, Nonlinear Programming Codes. VIII, 242 pages. 1980.

Vol. 184: R. E. Burkard and U. Derigs, Assignment and Matching Problems: Solution Methods with FORTRAN-Programs. VIII, 148 pages. 1980.

Vol. 185: C. C. von Weizsäcker, Barriers to Entry. VI, 220 pages. 1980.

Vol. 186: Ch.-L. Hwang and K. Yoon, Multiple Attribute Decision Making – Methods and Applications. A State-of-the-Art-Survey. XI, 259 pages. 1981.

Vol. 187: W. Hock, K. Schittkowski, Test Examples for Nonlinear Programming Codes. V. 178 pages. 1981.

Vol. 188: D. Bös, Economic Theory of Public Enterprise. VII, 142 pages. 1981.

Vol. 189: A. P. Lüthi, Messung wirtschaftlicher Ungleichheit. IX, 287 pages. 1981.

Vol. 190: J. N. Morse, Organizations: Multiple Agents with Multiple Criteria. Proceedings, 1980. VI, 509 pages. 1981.

Vol. 191: H. R. Sneessens, Theory and Estimation of Macroeconomic Rationing Models. VII, 138 pages. 1981.

Vol. 192: H. J. Bierens: Robust Methods and Asymptotic Theory in Nonlinear Econometrics. IX, 198 pages. 1981.

Vol. 193: J. K. Sengupta, Optimal Decisions under Uncertainty. VII, 156 pages. 1981.

Vol. 194: R. W. Shephard, Cost and Production Functions. XI, 104 pages. 1981.

Vol. 195: H. W. Ursprung, Die elementare Katastrophentheorie. Eine Darstellung aus der Sicht der Ökonomie. VII, 332 pages. 1982.

Vol. 196: M. Nermuth, Information Structures in Economics. VIII, 236 pages. 1982.

Vol. 197: Integer Programming and Related Areas. A Classified Bibliography. 1978 – 1981. Edited by R. von Randow. XIV, 338 pages. 1982.

Vol. 198: P. Zweifel, Ein ökonomisches Modell des Arztverhaltens. XIX, 392 Seiten. 1982.

Vol. 199: Evaluating Mathematical Programming Techniques. Proceedings, 1981. Edited by J.M. Mulvey. XI, 379 pages. 1982.

Vol. 200: The Resource Sector in an Open Economy. Edited by H. Siebert. IX, 161 pages. 1984.

Vol. 201: P. M. C. de Boer, Price Effects in Input-Output-Relations: A Theoretical and Empirical Study for the Netherlands 1949–1967. X, 140 pages. 1982.

Vol. 202: U. Witt, J. Perske, SMS – A Program Package for Simulation and Gaming of Stochastic Market Processes and Learning Behavior. VII, 266 pages. 1982.

Vol. 203: Compilation of Input-Output Tables. Proceedings, 1981. Edited by J. V. Skolka. VII, 307 pages. 1982.

Vol. 204: K.C. Mosler, Entscheidungsregeln bei Risiko: Multivariate stochastische Dominanz. VII, 172 Seiten. 1982.

Vol. 205: R. Ramanathan, Introduction to the Theory of Economic Growth. IX, 347 pages. 1982.

Vol. 206: M.H. Karwan, V. Lotfi, J. Telgen, and S. Zionts, Redundancy in Mathematical Programming. VII, 286 pages. 1983.

Vol. 207: Y. Fujimori, Modern Analysis of Value Theory. X, 165 pages. 1982.

Vol. 208: Econometric Decision Models. Proceedings, 1981. Edited by J. Gruber. VI, 364 pages. 1983.

Vol. 209: Essays and Surveys on Multiple Criteria Decision Making. Proceedings, 1982. Edited by P. Hansen. VII, 441 pages. 1983.

Vol. 210: Technology, Organization and Economic Structure. Edited by R. Sato and M.J. Beckmann. VIII, 195 pages. 1983.

continuation on page 157

Lecture Notes
in Economics and
Mathematical Systems

Managing Editors: M. Beckmann and W. Krelle

313

Werner Jammernegg

Sequential Binary Investment Decisions

A Bayesian Approach

Springer-Verlag
Berlin Heidelberg New York London Paris Tokyo

Author

Dr. Werner Jammernegg
Institut für Statistik, Ökonometrie und Operations Research
Karl-Franzens-Universität Graz
Herdergasse 11, A-8010 Graz, Austria

ISBN-13: 978-3-540-50034-6 e-ISBN-13: 978-3-642-46646-5
DOI: 10.1007/978-3-642-46646-5

2142/3140-543210

Preface

This book describes some models from the theory of investment which are mainly characterized by three features. Firstly, the decision–maker acts in a dynamic environment. Secondly, the distributions of the random variables are only incompletely known at the beginning of the planning process. This is termed as decision–making under conditions of uncertainty. Thirdly, in large parts of the work we restrict the analysis to binary decision models. In a binary model, the decision–maker must choose one of two actions. For example, one decision means to undertake the investment project in a planning period, whereas the other decision prescribes to postpone the project for at least one more period.

The analysis of dynamic decision models under conditions of uncertainty is not a very common approach in economics. In this framework the optimal decisions are only obtained by the extensive use of methods from operations research and from statistics. It is the intention to narrow some of the existing gaps in the fields of investment and portfolio analysis in this respect. This is done by combining techniques that have been developed in investment theory and portfolio selection, in stochastic dynamic programming, and in Bayesian statistics. The latter field indicates the use of Bayes' theorem for the revision of the probability distributions of the random variables over time.

The book is divided into four chapters. Chapter 1 introduces the basic concept of decision–making under uncertainty and explains how risk–aversion and uncertainty are incorporated in the binary investment models. The first chapter is concluded by a brief summary of the remaining part of the work. Chapter 2 puts together the probabilistic and statistical results that are used later on. The main tool is the concept of monotone transition probabilities. Chapter 3 is devoted to the analysis of dynamic two–asset portfolio models. Such a portfolio model is called binary if in each planning period the decision–maker must invest all the initial wealth in only one asset. Chapter 4 deals with the determination of the optimal investment date of an irreversible real project over a finite planning horizon.

This book is the slightly revised and translated version of my Habilitationsschrift that has been accepted by the Faculty of Economics and Social Sciences of the University of Graz in June 1987. It is a pleasure to express my sincere gratitude to Professors Jochen Hülsmann, Angelien Kemna, Klaus Spremann, Peter Swoboda, and Jochen Wilhelm and to my colleagues and friends Edwin Fischer, Peter Steiner, and Professor

Josef Zechner for stimulating comments and valuable suggestions at various stages of this work.

My special appreciation belongs to Professor Peter Kischka for many discussions concerning the chapter on dynamic portfolio models. My greatest debt of gratitude goes to Harald Benzing for the cooperation in the field of dynamic binary decision models. Section 4.4 of this book on investment timing models under uncertainty is based on a joint working paper with Harald.

Finally, I wish to give my thanks to Professor Ulrich Dieter for the permission to use the text processing facilities at his department, and particularly to Ulli Fleischhacker and Hillo Grabl–Ruttner for the excellent typing of the English and of the German manuscript. In addition, I would like to acknowledge the excellent cooperation with Werner A. Müller and Marianne Bopp from Springer–Verlag.

Graz, April 1988 Werner Jammernegg

Contents

1. Introduction

The main intention of this book is to develop simple dynamic models in which decision–makers, e.g. private investors or managers of firms, have to make sequential decisions under conditions of uncertainty. Sequential decision processes are the appropriate tool for the analysis of economic behaviour from a theoretical point of view and provide also a valid description of empirical decision–making.

There is, however, still a lack of truly dynamic models in economic theory. In many of these dynamic models only myopic decision rules or certainty equivalence rules are derived instead. Also probabilistic analysis is not a very common approach. One reason for this lack is that economic theory usually tries to explain the behaviour of representative decision– makers but not the behaviour of individual decision–makers (cp. Lippman/ McCall (1981), p. 213). Another reason for the significance of deterministic models is their popularity in practice. There the necessity for simplifications often can be observed (cp. Bamberg/Coenenberg (1985), p. 39).

But the information accumulation that characterizes a sequential decision process is neglected not only by a purly deterministic model but also by a model under conditions of risk. We distinguish between a decision model under conditions of risk and a decision model under conditions of uncertainty on the basis of the knowledge about the probability distributions of the stochastic variables. For the decision model under risk all probability distributions can be specified at the beginning of the planning process. In a decision model under uncertainty the decision–maker is assumed to know only the families of probability distributions. A simple example of such a situation is that one or more parameters of the distribution are unknown. This distinction between risk and uncertainty goes back to Knight and is used throughout this work (cp. Cyert/De Groot (1987), p. 3, Jones/Ostroy (1984), p. 24).

The concept of learning is a fundamental tool for sequential decision making. Learning, however, can only be achieved through additional observations. Therefore, the dynamic decision model under conditions of risk is not an appropriate framework if the (individual) decision–maker wants to revise his knowledge and beliefs during the planning process. Because the probability distributions are fixed, learning cannot take place in this situation.

A powerful framework to develop this concept of learning in a dynamic model is the Bayesian approach (cp. Cyert/De Groot (1987), preface, Firchau (1986), p. 8 and p. 16). To a Bayesian decision–maker all uncertainty can be represented by probability distributions. Consequently, all unknown parameters of the probability distributions can be assigned (subjective) prior distributions. But in economics the concept of subjective probability is still relatively uncommon in sequential decision making. We are convinced, however, that the Bayesian approach is also an appropriate tool for information processing in economics.

In this work the framework of dynamic Bayesian decision models is used for the formulation and for the analysis of investment processes. A drawback in dynamic decision–making is the discrepancy between the empirical validity of the model and the possibility to obtain powerful results. Therefore, in large parts of the work we focus on such cases which can be represented by only two alternate actions, namely on binary dynamic decision models.

We present a dynamic portfolio model consisting of two assets in the above framework, and we use a stopping decision model to analyze the determination of the construction date of long–lived investment projects. We concentrate on the derivation of qualitative results which, of course, cannot be interpreted as recommendation how to act. Our intentions are much more pragmatic: For the decision–situations considered, we want to explain simple economic behaviour which often can be observed in practice. One prominent example is the stop–loss strategy.

Until now we have only described the risk attitudes of the decision–maker in the form of the concept of subjective probability, i.e. the Bayesian approach. But from the point of view of statistical decision theory we have to say something about the decision–maker's risk preferences in the form of a utility function. For the binary decision models discussed in this work we choose another way of incorporating the risk preferences of the decision maker in the model. This is the subject of the following section.

1.1 Uncertainty and Risk Aversion

In individual investment analysis two different approaches to represent a decision–maker's preferences and beliefs over strategies which yield random reward are in wide use. Under the mean–variance approach the decision–maker is assumed to rank the alternatives according to the first two moments of the random reward, e.g. the final wealth. This approach has a long tradition in portfolio selection. In this framework a portfolio dominates another if its expected final wealth is higher and its variance of final wealth is lower than the corresponding quantities of the other portfolio. The expected utility principle, however, ranks the alternatives according to the expected value of some specified utility function of the random reward. The expected utility framework, dating back to the work of Bernoulli, is the classic decision criterion in statistical decision theory. For a recent comparison of these two approaches we refer to the paper of Meyer (1987).

Whereas the decision-maker's subjective probabilities represent his knowledge and beliefs, the utility represents the tastes and the preference of the decision-maker. Therefore, risk or uncertainty are expressed by probability distributions, but risk preferences are usually characterized by utility functions. Risk-averse behaviour is considered by the specification of a concave utility function whereas risk-taking behaviour corresponds to a convex utility function. A risk-neutral decision-maker is described, of course, by a linear utility function in the expected utility framework.

In portfolio analysis, however, risk-neutrality, i.e. a linear utility function, leads to an unrealistic result: If the investor can choose between several risky assets, he will put his whole wealth into that asset which guarantees the highest expected return. Thus, a risk-neutral investor does not hold a diversified portfolio which would cause a reduction of the variance of the final wealth by investing in several risky assets.

We are mainly concerned with the analysis of binary dynamic investment models under conditions of uncertainty. In this way learning is incorporated in the sequential approach, i.e. the decision in each planning period is designed to gather information that is useful for the decisions in subsequent periods. Because this type of model provides a basis for empirical decision-making, the decision criterion also should be of empirical relevance.

Several experimental studies showed a lack of empirical validity of the mean-variance approach. The data generated from the experiments also did not fit to some often used utility functions, like the quadratic, logarithmic or power utilities. It is not surprising to us that in fact all moments of the probability distributions influence the risk attitudes of the investors (cp. Barua/Srinivasan (1987), pp. 247).

In their work Barua/Srinivasan (1987) investigated the empirical evidence for three decision criteria: the mean-variance approach, the stochastic dominance approach and an approach based on the mean, the variance and the skewness of the random variable. The participants in the experiment had to choose between six alternate portfolios which are composed of a risky and a riskless asset over a finite but unknown planning horizon. The distribution of the risky asset in any case was asymmetric.

The result of the experiment showed that only a quarter of the participants behaved in accordance with the mean–variance criterion. Approximately half of the choices conformed to the stochastic dominance rule. Thus, in this experiment the preferences of the individuals have not been explained adequately either by the stochastic dominance rule or by the mean–variance framework.

Consequently, Barua and Srinivasan searched for an alternate criterion, the mean–variance–skewness criterion. If in this framework two alternative decisions have the same mean and variance, then the one with the higher skewness is preferred. Of course, the alternative with the lower variance is preferred in case the mean and the skewness are identical. If two alternative decisions have the same variance and skewness, then the one with the higher mean clearly is chosen.

Three quarters of the choices that violated the mean–variance rule were in accordance with this criterion. Therefore, the inclusion of skewness of the risky asset provided a much better explanation of the decisions made in the experiment. The participants showed a significant preference for positive skewness at all levels of wealth (cp. Barua/Srinivasan (1987), pp. 251).

What conclusions can be drawn from this experimental study ? It is common experience that decision–makers behave in general risk–averse or at most risk–neutral. Thus, we can assume that the participants in the experiment are more or less risk–averters. Although the participants have not explicitly been asked about their utility assessments, the dominance of the mean–variance–skewness criterion over the classic mean–variance criterion shows that only a part of the risk–averse behaviour is explained by the utility function. A decisive part of the risk–averse behaviour is expressed by the positive skewness of the risky asset. This seems to be a modest indication that the probability distribution of a stochastic variable does express not only the decision–maker's degree of uncertainty but also his degree of risk aversion, provided the distribution is positively skewed (cp. e.g. Jones/Ostroy (1984), p. 24).

Of course, the previous discussion by no means has the intention to question the merits of the expected utility framework. We just wanted to state that for the analysis of the binary portfolio model in section 3.2, where diversification in the usual sense is not allowed, the risk–averse behaviour of the investor can be taken into consideration not only by a concave utility function but also by probability distributions with positive skewness. There we will perform numerical sensitivity investigations which show the effects on the optimal investment decisions if the utility function and the distribution of the risky asset, respectively, is changed.

We conclude the introductory remarks with the following citation which reflects our intentions quite well: "But, though in many circumstances risk aversion is a fact and is essential to understanding economic behaviour, much economic behavior is a direct consequence of uncertainty and is independent of risk aversion" (Lippman/Mc Call (1981), p. 212). Contrary to the final part of this statement we think that to some extent risk aversion can be incorporated in the decision–maker's concept of uncertainty.

1.2 Methods and Organization

In this work we investigate binary dynamic decision models under conditions of uncertainty in investment and portfolio theory. As general method of analysis we use the so–called structured dynamic programming which is a special case of stochastic dynamic programming. There the specific structure of the model allows to derive qualitative properties of the optimal decision functions, like e.g. monotonicity. Up to now only general assumptions for the value functions of dynamic programming exist (cp. Serfozo (1976), Heyman/Sobel (1984), chapter 8).

But in many situations this general approach is not successful as we will see in the course of the analysis of the portfolio models. Therefore, we restrict the attention to stochastic dynamic programs with only two decisions. The assumptions of the basic investment or portfolio model are used to formulate the corresponding dynamic program. The special structure of this dynamic program then is exploited to demonstrate the previously mentioned qualitative properties of the optimal decisions.

The essential characteristics of the dynamic program are the reward functions and the transition probabilities. In chapter two we are mainly concerned with the qualitative properties of these transition probabilities, with so–called monotone transition probabilities. Because we are discussing investment and portfolio models under conditions of uncertainty, only the families of the probability distributions of the stochastic model variables are known. For the matter of presentation we limit ourselves to just one unknown parameter of these distributions. Furthermore, we consider only the family of the Bernoulli, the Normal, the Lognormal, and the Gamma distributions. The Lognormal and the Gamma distributions always have positive skewness. The unknown parameter is revised by the information obtained over time. Because this revision is done by means of the Bayesian approach, the specification of a prior distribution for the unknown parameter is also necessary. The decision-maker can use the prior distribution to express his knowledge and his subjective beliefs.

The main concern of chapter two is to show that the Bayesian information processing just leads to monotone transition probabilities with respect to the information state obtained over time. When we start from the prior distribution, the resulting posterior distribution then is shown to be a monotone transition probability.

In chapter three we are dealing with the analysis of discrete-time dynamic portfolio models over a finite planning horizon. We restrict to two assets, one riskless asset and one risky asset. If there are more than two assets, almost no qualitative results of the optimal investment decisions can be obtained.

We start with the analysis of the portfolio model under conditions of risk, that is the return distribution of the risky asset is assumed to be known in advance for all planning periods. The aim of the decision-maker is the maximization of the expected utility of final wealth at the planning horizon. If the returns of the risky asset are stochastically independent over time, we derive the characteristics of the optimal investment decisions. As we allow for diversification in the usual sense, we term this type of portfolio model as classic.

In the next step we abandon the assumption of stochastically independent returns over time for these classic portfolio models. Afterwards we devote to the analysis of the classic dynamic portfolio model under conditions of uncertainty. We assume indeed that the returns of the risky asset are independent but that their probability distributions depend on an unknown parameter. Bayes' Theorem is used to revise the return distribution by means of the observed returns. Unfortunately, for this kind of portfolio model all qualitative properties of the optimal investment decisions, like the monotonicity with respect to the initial wealth of a planning period or with respect to the information state, are lost.

This is one important reason to switch at this point from the classic dynamic portfolio model to the binary dynamic portfolio model. In the latter one only diversification over time is allowed. The decision–maker must invest the whole initial wealth of a planning period exclusively in one of the two assets. The goal of the investor again is the maximization of the expected utility of final wealth at the planning horizon. But we limit the analysis in this case to utility functions with constant relative risk–aversion in the sense of Arrow/Pratt. As a consequence, the optimal investment decisions do not depend on the initial wealth of a planning period. We focus, however, on the linear utility function. The risk–attitudes of the investor then are only expressed by the return distributions with positive skewness.

We consider exclusively the so–called stop–loss strategies which are widely employed, not only by small investors but also by large institutions. In order to characterize this strategy, we assume that in the first planning period the investor decides for the risky asset. In each of the subsequent periods the investor checks this decision by including the already observed returns. Once the optimal decision rule says to return to the riskless asset, the investor stays away from risky assets for a while. In the model this is expressed by the assumption that in such a situation the investor stops observing the returns of the risky asset.

This kind of behaviour is known from the one–armed–bandit models which are also applied in other fields of economic theory, like in the field of search models (cp. Berninghaus (1984)). A survey of bandit models is contained in Berry/Fristedt (1985).

The optimal investment decisions of the binary dynamic portfolio model have a number of structural properties. Firstly, we show that the stop–loss strategy is indeed optimal; in other words we show that the so–called stopping rule holds. Secondly, the optimal investment decisions are monotone functions with respect to the information state. Thirdly, the stay–on–a–winner rule holds provided the return distribution of the risky asset is a two–point distribution: If in a planning period the investor puts the money into the risky asset and if he realizes the "high" return, then in the subsequent period it is optimal to invest again in the risky asset.

We conclude chapter three with several numerical sensitivity investigations. We are first of all interested in the effects on the optimal investment decisions if the utility function and the prior distribution of the unknown parameter of the return distribution are varied.

In chapter four we deal with the determination of the optimal investment date of an irreversible project over a finite planning horizon. We do not raise the question what project should be invested, but we raise the question when an already fixed investment project should be undertaken.

As we have already mentioned, the latter question is relevant for long–lived investment projects in any case. Therefore, this concerns first of all real investments, like machine tools, where it is not sufficient to make the decision to invest according to the usual net–present–value–rule. Investment in an irreversible project is only optimal if the net present value exceeds a positive number, the so–called net–present–value–premium (cp. e.g. Baldwin/Meyer (1979)).

We analyze a real investment project which is traded on the capital market. Thus, in each planning period the market value of the project can be observed. We begin with the presentation of a deterministic model and we carry out sensitivity investigations with respect to the market interest rate. Afterwards we develop an investment model under conditions of risk. The goal of the investor is to maximize the discounted expected market value of the project. We assume that the probability distribution of the market value is known for all periods at the beginning of the planning process. We show that the optimal investment decisions are monotone functions of the market value. Then we compare our discrete–time model with already known models for the determination of the optimal investment date. The major part of these models is designed in continuous time with an infinite planning horizon. The market value often follows a diffusion process, in particular a geometric Wiener process. Therefore, this type of models is sometimes referred to as "diffusion models".

Finally, we turn to a model for the determination of the optimal investment date under conditions of uncertainty. There we assume that the distribution of the market value depends on an unknown parameter. For this parameter in a Bayesian manner an a priori distribution can be specified. The posterior distribution of the market value then is computed by taking into consideration the observed market values of the project.

This model is described as a binary stopping decision model and is analyzed by means of dynamic programming techniques. The decision–maker, e.g. the manager of a firm, must choose between two actions. The decision to stop prescribes to undertake the investment project in the running period. The decision to continue means that the project is postponed at least for one more period if the planning horizon has not yet been reached.

We show that in this framework the optimal investment decisions are monotone functions of the information state. Afterwards we perform extensive sensitivity analyses. Among other things we demonstrate that the variation of the market interest rate may lead to a sensitivity result which is in contrast to that of the deterministic model; the value of a risk parameter decides the matter for the effect on the optimal investment decision. Futhermore, we compare the optimal investment policy with the certainty equivalence policy which is obtained if the stochastic market values are replaced by the respective posterior expected market values.

Finally, we point at another potential application of this investment–timing–model in the field of financial assets, namely the determination of the optimal excercise date of an American call option. It is well known from the theory of option pricing that it is never optimal to exercise the option before its expiration date provided the underlying stock pays no dividends during the time to maturity of the option.

Contrary to known option models we assume that the exercise price of the option is not invested at the riskless interest rate until its exercise. This means that in our model only for the case of no discounting it is optimal to exercise the option only at the expiration date. If, however, the market interest rate is positive, then in general it is optimal to make use of the right to exercise the option before its expiration date.

In chapter five the work is concluded with some brief remarks concerning possible extensions of the presented models.

2. The Monotonicity of Transition Probabilities

Consider the following situation: The return of a risky asset, say a stock, is characterized by the probability distribution (*pd*) ν_θ that depends on the unknown parameter $\theta \in \Theta \subseteq \mathbf{R}$. Now suppose the investor observes the returns $(r_1, \ldots, r_k)$ as time evolves. Thus, he is confronted with the question whether it is necessary to know the whole vector of returns $(r_1, \ldots, r_k)$ for the determination (estimation) of parameter θ – one may think of the amount of data that has to be stored if the number of observed returns is growing – , or whether it is enough to know just a condensed form of this vector of observations. This problem is addressed in the first section using the concept of sufficient statistics for the considered *pd*.

As we are starting in this work from a Bayesian point of view, the estimation of θ is based not only on the sample $(r_1, \ldots, r_k)$ but also on the specification of a prior *pd* for the unknown parameter $\theta \in \Theta$. Having in mind the concept of conjugate distributions, the computational complexity of the resulting posterior distribution is considerably reduced. This concept means that prior and posterior *pd* for parameter θ are members of the same familiy of distributions.

Of special importance are structural properties as e.g. monotonicity of the optimal investment policy of the models discussed in the following chapters. It is thus necessary to define monotone transition probabilities (*tp*) as a natural extension of stochastic dominance. Monotone *tp* are essentially characterized by the monotone likelihood ratio property of the return distribution ν_θ, $\theta \in \Theta$ (section 2).

2.1 Sufficient Statistics

Let for the following $X = (X_1, \ldots, X_n)$ be a (random) sample of size n, where $X_1, \ldots, X_n$ are *iid* real random variables with common *pd* ν_θ for fixed parameter $\theta \in \Theta \subseteq \mathbf{R}$. The sample space of $X_i, 1 \leq i \leq n$, is denoted by $\mathcal{X}$. We are now faced with the problem, starting from a realization $(x_1, \ldots, x_n)$ of the sample X to determine an estimate for θ and therewith for the *pd* for the random variables $X_i, 1 \leq i \leq n$.

Apart from the fact that it might become more and more expensive to store the data as the sample size n is growing, the realization of the sample $(x_1, \ldots, x_n)$ will often not be suitable for computing an estimate of the parameter θ. Thus, it is our goal to find a statistic $T(X)$ of the sample X that will condense the data. Furthermore it will be desirable that $T(X)$ is of constant dimension, which means that the dimension of $T(X)$ does not vary with the sample size. Of course, we have to take notice of losing no information by making this transformation. This means that the value of information which is contained in the statistic $T(X)$ is the same as the value of information of the original sample X. Such statistics are termed sufficient (see for this topic Lehmann (1983), pp. 36, Rohatgi (1976), pp. 338, Berger (1985), pp. 35).

Before presenting the sufficient statistics for the considered distributions, namely the Bernoulli, Normal, Lognormal and Gamma distribution, we give a formal definition.

DEFINITION 2.1. *Let $X = (X_1, \ldots, X_n)$ be a sample, where $X_1, \ldots, X_n$ are iid random variables with common pd ν_θ, $\theta \in \Theta$. A statistic $Y := T(X)$ is sufficient for $\theta, \theta \in \Theta$, if and only if the conditional distribution of X, given Y and θ, does not depend on the parameter $\theta \in \Theta$.*

In general it might be a difficult task to compute the conditional distribution of X, given $Y = y$, in order to check the sufficiency of statistic $Y = T(X)$.

We denote the probability mass function (density function) of the discrete (continuous) random variable $X = (X_1, \ldots, X_n)$ with $f_\theta(x)$, $(x_1, \ldots, x_n) \in \mathcal{X}^n$, $\theta \in \Theta$. Then the factorization criterion of Neyman–Fisher gives a necessary and sufficient condition for the sufficiency of statistic T in terms of $f_\theta(x)$:

THEOREM 2.2. *Let $X = (X_1, \ldots, X_n)$ be a discrete (continuous) random variable with probability mass function (density function) $f_\theta(x)$, $x \in \mathcal{X}^n$, $\theta \in \Theta$. A statistic $T(X)$ is sufficient for θ if and only if there exist nonnegative functions g_θ, $h: \mathcal{X}^n \to \mathbf{R}^+$, such that we have for all $\theta \in \Theta$:*

$$f_\theta(x) = g_\theta(T(x))\, h(x)\,. \tag{2,1}$$

For a proof of this theorem see e.g. Rohatgi (1976), pp. 341. It is crucial that the function h is independent of θ and that g_θ depends on x only via T.

2.1.1. Sufficient Statistics for One-parameter Exponential Families

A common feature of the *pd* which characterize in this work the market value or the return of an investment is the fact that they belong to a so-called exponential family of distributions.

DEFINITION 2.3. *A parametric family of pd's is a (one-parameter) exponential family, if the corresponding probability mass function or density function* $\bar{f}_\theta(x)$, $x \in \mathcal{X}$, *is for all* $\theta \in \Theta$ *of the following form:*

$$\bar{f}_\theta(x) = a(\theta)\, h(x) \exp[t(x) b(\theta)] \,. \tag{2,2}$$

a, h, t *and* b *are real-valued functions.*

For the sample $X = (X_1, \ldots, X_n)$ with probability mass function (density) $f_\theta(x_1, \ldots, x_n) = \bar{f}_\theta(x_1) \cdot \ldots \cdot \bar{f}_\theta(x_n)$ we have immediately for $x = (x_1, \ldots, x_n) \in \mathcal{X}^n$ and $\theta \in \Theta$:

$$f_\theta(x) = A(\theta)\, H(x) \exp\left[T(x) b(\theta)\right] , \tag{2,3}$$

where $A(\theta) := a(\theta)^n$, $H(x) := h(x_1) \cdot \ldots \cdot h(x_n)$, $T(x) = t(x_1) + \cdots + t(x_n)$. From (2,3) we conclude the following: if the *pd* of the random variables X_i, $1 \le i \le n$, belong to a one-parameter exponential family, then the *pd* of $X = (X_1, \ldots, X_n)$ is also a member of a one-parameter exponential family.

A comparison of (2,3) with the factorization criterion for sufficient statistics (2,1) leads to a result that is important for our purposes:

COROLLARY 2.4. *If the pd of the random variables* X_i, $1 \le i \le n$, *belong to a one-parameter exponential family with parameter* θ, *then* $T(x)$, *given by* (2,3), *is a one-dimensional sufficient statistic for* θ , $\theta \in \Theta$.

Because we are restricting our attention to *pd* that are members of a one-parameter exponential family (2,2), the statement of the corollary means not only that there exists a sufficient statistic T whose dimension is independent of the sample size, but also that T is moreover one-dimensional.

In Table 2.1 we present some special discrete and continuous distributions. As can be checked easily, they are all members of a one-parameter exponential family. Besides its functional form, the table contains the name and the abbreviation of the probability mass function and density function, respectively. Furthermore it shows the support $\mathcal{X}$, the set Θ of possible values of the unknown parameter θ, the (minimal) sufficient statistic $Y = T(X)$ for a sample of size n as well as the name of the probability mass function (density function) of T.

As can be seen from the last column of Table 2.1, the *pd* of the sufficient statistic $T(X)$ also belongs to a one-parameter exponential family. Moreover this fact is true in general (see e.g. Rohatgi (1976), p. 238).

Table 2.1:
Sufficient statistics of special distributions of the one–parameter exponential type.

probability mass function or density function	name and abbreviation	$\mathcal{X}$	Θ	$Y = T(X)$	*pd* of T
$\theta^x(1-\theta)^{1-x}$	Bernoulli $b(1,\theta)$	$\{0,1\}$	$(0,1)$	$Y = \sum_{i=1}^n X_i$	$b(n,\theta)$
$\frac{x^{\alpha-1}\theta^\alpha}{\Gamma(\alpha)}e^{-\theta x}$	Gamma $G(\alpha,\theta)$	$\mathbf{R}^+$	$\mathbf{R}^+$	$Y = \sum_{i=1}^n X_i$	$G(n\alpha,\theta)$
$\frac{1}{\sqrt{2\pi}\sigma}\exp\left(-\frac{(x-\theta)^2}{2\sigma^2}\right)$	Normal $N(\theta,\sigma^2)$	$\mathbf{R}$	$\mathbf{R}$	$Y = \sum_{i=1}^n X_i$	$N(n\theta,n\sigma^2)$
$\frac{1}{\sqrt{2\pi}\sigma x}\exp\left(-\frac{(\log x-\theta)^2}{2\sigma^2}\right)$	Lognormal $LN(\theta,\sigma^2)$	$\mathbf{R}^+$	$\mathbf{R}$	$Y = \prod_{i=1}^n X_i$	$LN(n\theta,n\sigma^2)$

2.2 Posterior Distributions and Transition Probabilities

We have just seen that for the distributions from Table 2.1 one–dimensional sufficient statistics exist. If the decision-maker observes the sample-realization $(x_1,\ldots,x_n)$ of size n, he has just to remember the number of observations n and the realization of the sufficient statistic $y = T(x_1,\ldots,x_n)$. Therefore in the following the pair (n,y) will be denoted as information state of the decision–maker.

Apart from the previously mentioned "objective" information characterized by the information state (n,y) additionally we take the "subjective" beliefs of the decision-maker into consideration. When we start from a Bayesian point of view, this is achieved by specifying a prior distribution $\overline{\mu}$ for the unknown parameter θ. In this way it is possible to indicate the risk attitudes by assertion of the prior moments of the distribution, as e.g. the expected value, the variance, the skewness and the kurtosis. This seems to be a possibility of avoiding the specification of a (concave) utility function, by which in decision theory risk-averse behaviour of decision-makers is usually expressed. We shall return to this important question and thereby to the choice of the *pd* presented in Table 2.1 in course of the discussion of the portfolio-model in chapter 3.

2.2.1 Definitions and Basic Properties

We denote in the following the probability mass function and density function, respectively, of the sufficient statistic $Y := T(X_1, \ldots, X_n)$ in dependence on the unknown parameter θ by $g(n, y; \theta)$, where (n, y) is the given information state.

Starting from the prior distribution $\overline{\mu}$, the posterior distribution for parameter θ is characterized according to the theorem of Bayes by the following transition probability (*tp*):

$$\mu(n, y; D) := \int_D g(n, y; \theta)\overline{\mu}(d\theta) \Big/ \int_\Theta g(n, y; \theta')\overline{\mu}(d\theta') \quad \text{for } n \in \mathbf{N}$$

(2,4)

$$\mu(n, y; D) := \overline{\mu}(D) \quad \text{for} \quad n = 0\,,$$

where $D \subseteq \Theta$.

Thus, we are in the position to specify the posterior distribution of the random variable X_{n+1}, e.g. the random return in period $n+1$, for given information state (n, y) also as a *tp*:

$$p(n, y; B) := \int_\Theta \nu_\theta(B)\mu(n, y;\, d\theta)\,, \quad B \subseteq \mathcal{X}\,, \tag{2,5}$$

where ν_θ represents the *pd* of X_{n+1} in dependence on parameter θ.

Now we define for all functions $U : \mathcal{X} \to \mathbf{R}$, whose integral with respect to *tp* p from (2,5) exists, the conditional expectation, given (n, y):

$$u(n, y) := \int_{\mathcal{X}} U(x)\, p(n, y;\, dx)\,. \tag{2,6}$$

Furthermore, we see from Table 2.1 that for these distributions the sufficient statistic $Y = T(X_1, \ldots, X_n)$ can be determined in a recursive way, namely:

$$(2,7) \qquad T(X_1, \ldots, X_{n+1}) = v(T(X_1, \ldots, X_n), X_{n+1}) = v(Y, X_{n+1}).$$

The recursion function $v(y,x)$ is given by either $v(y,x) = y+x$ or $v(y,x) = yx$ (in case of the Lognormal distribution).

This leads to a result which can be easily understood from intuition:

THEOREM 2.5. *For all information states* $(n,y) \in \mathbf{N}_0 \times \mathbf{R}$ *we have:*

$$\int_{\mathcal{X}} u(n+1\,,\ v(y,x))\ p(n,y;\ dx) = u(n,y)\,.$$

For a proof see Benzing/Kolonko (1987), Lemma 4.1.

If we interpret U as utility function, the assertion of Theorem 2.5 has the following meaning: When we start from information state (n,y), the expected utility for $n+1$ observations is the same as the expected utility computed from n realizations.

2.2.2 Monotone Transition Probabilities

In (2,4) and (2,5) the posterior distributions of the parameter θ and of the random variable X[1] have been represented as *tp*. In order to demonstrate qualitative results like monotonicity of the optimal investment decisions as a function of the information state, it is necessary to classify these *tp* in some sense also with respect to the information state. This is achieved by so–called monotone *tp* that essentially represent a generalization of the well–known concept of stochastic dominance (or monotonicity) (for the latter see e.g. Stoyan (1983), pp. 4).

Before this can be done, we must be able to classify the information states $(n,y) \in \mathbf{N}_0 \times \mathbf{R}$ in a reasonable way. In the following two information states (n,y) and (n',y') are compared by means of relation " $\leq$":

$$(2,8) \qquad (n,y) \leq (n',y') \quad \text{if and only if} \quad n = n' \quad \text{and} \quad y \leq y'\,.$$

[1]In the remaining part of this chapter the random variable X_n in period n is simply denoted by X.

Information state (n', y') contains better information compared with (n, y) if the sufficient statistic Y yields the higher value y' – e.g. the cumulative returns or market values y' are higher than y –, provided that the number of observations is the same in both information states, i.e. $n = n'$.

In the case of a Bernoulli distribution, or more general a two–point distribution, it is reasonable to enlarge relation "$\leq$" from (2,8) in the following way:

(2,8') $\quad (n, y) \leq (n', y')$ if and only if $\quad y \leq y' \quad$ and $\quad n - y \geq n' - y'$.

Assume that realization 1 of the distribution describes success and the observation of the high return of a risky asset, respectively, and realization 0 denotes failure and observation of the low return, respectively. Then relation (2,8') states that information state (n', y') is better than (n, y) as it contains more successes $(y' \geq y)$ and at the same time less failures $(n' - y' \leq n - y)$; or in other words: because in comparison more high returns and less low returns have been realized.

Now we are in the position to define a monotone *tp*; we are doing this by means of the posterior distribution for X from (2,5); the same procedure holds for the *tp* μ of parameter θ from (2,4).

DEFINITION 2.6. *The transition probability p from $\mathbf{N}_0 \times \mathbf{R}$ to $\mathcal{X}$ is monotone if and only if*

$$p(n, y; B) \leq p(n', y'; B)$$

for all $(n, y), (n', y') \in \mathbf{N}_0 \times \mathbf{R}$ where $(n, y) \leq (n', y')$ and for all increasing sets $B \subseteq \mathcal{X}$[2].

If $p(n, y; B) \geq p(n', y'; B)$ holds, the tp is called antimonotone.

The following theorem presents a practical criterion for the characterization of monotone *tp*:

THEOREM 2.7. *Let p be a tp from $\mathbf{N}_0 \times \mathbf{R}$ to $\mathcal{X}$.*
Then the following statements are equivalent:

a) *p is a monotone tp.*
b) *$\int_{\mathcal{X}} f(x) p(n, y; dx)$ is nondecreasing (nonincreasing) in (n, y) for each nondecreasing (nonincreasing) function $f : \mathcal{X} \to \mathbf{R}$, for which the integral with respect to p exists.*

---

[2] A set $B \subseteq \mathcal{X} \subseteq \mathbf{R}$ is called increasing, if for $x_1, x_2 \in \mathcal{X}$ and $x_1 \leq x_2$ we have that $x_1 \in B$ implies $x_2 \in B$.

For a proof see Serfozo (1976), Corollary 4.2.

A similar result holds for antimonotone *tp*:

COROLLARY 2.8. *Let p be a tp from* $\mathbf{N}_0 \times \mathbf{R}$ *to* $\mathcal{X}$.
Then the following statements are equivalent.

a) *p is an antimonotone tp.*
b) $\int_{\mathcal{X}} f(x)p(n,y;\,dx)$ *is nonincreasing (nondecreasing) in* (n,y) *for each nondecreasing (nonincreasing) function* $f: \mathcal{X} \to \mathbf{R}$, *for which the integral with respect to p exists.*

We are now approaching the main result of this chapter. The goal is to show that for the distributions considered in Table 2.1 the posterior distributions for the unknown parameter θ and for the random variable X are in fact monotone and antimonotone *tp*, respectively. Starting–point is the monotonicity of the likelihood ratio of the probability mass function and density function $g(n,y;\theta)$, respectively, in the information state (n,y).

DEFINITION 2.9. *The family of probability mass functions (density functions)* $\{g(n,y;\theta),\ \theta \in \Theta\}$ *has an increasing (decreasing)* <u>*monotone likelihood ratio*</u> *(MLR) with respect to the information state* (n,y), *if for* $\theta, \theta' \in \Theta$ *where* $\theta < \theta'$ *the ratio* $g(n,y;\theta')/g(n,y;\theta)$ *is a nondecreasing (nonincreasing) function of* (n,y), *and that for all* $(n,y) \in \mathbf{N}_0 \times \mathbf{R}$, *for which either* $g(n,y;\theta) > 0$ *or* $g(n,y;\theta') > 0$ *holds.*

A good survey on the subject of MLR can be found in Rohatgi (1976), pp. 418.

We have concluded from Table 2.1 that the probability mass functions (density functions) of the sufficient statistics $Y = T(X_1, \ldots X_n)$ also belong to the class of one–parameter exponential families. In general, this can be represented in the following way:

$$g(n,y;\theta) = A(\theta)H^*(n,y)\exp\left(y \cdot b(\theta)\right), \tag{2,9}$$

where $H^*(n,y)$ has to be determined from $H(x_1,\ldots,x_n)$, defined in (2,3).

Therefore, the next result is immediately obtained:

LEMMA 2.10. *If the family of probability mass functions and density functions* $\{g(n,y;\theta),\ \theta \in \Theta\}$, *respectively, belongs to a one– parameter exponential family of the type (2,9), then this family has an increasing (decreasing) MLR in the information state* (n,y), *if* $\theta \to b(\theta)$ *is nondecreasing (nonincreasing).*

If the sufficient statistic $Y = T(X_1, \dots, X_n)$ has a Binomial $b(n, \theta)$, a Normal $N(n\theta; n\sigma^2)$ and a Lognormal $LN(n\theta, n\sigma^2)$ distribution, respectively, then $g(n, y; \theta)$ has an increasing MLR. In the case of a Gamma $G(n\alpha, \theta)$ distribution, the density $g(n, y; \theta)$ has a decreasing MLR.

This MLR–property of the family $\{g(n, y; \theta)\}$ is now used to show that the *tp* μ for the unknown parameter θ, as defined in (2,4), is monotone and antimonotone, respectively. For the following we exclude the (uninteresting) situation that the prior distribution $\overline{\mu}$ for θ is degenerated, i.e. a one–point distribution.

LEMMA 2.11. *Let $\{g(n, y; \theta)\}$ be a family of probability mass functions and density functions, respectively, with increasing (decreasing) MLR in the information state (n, y). Furthermore, let $\overline{\mu}$ be a nondegenerated prior distribution for parameter θ. The posterior distribution μ for θ then is a monotone (antimonotone) tp.*

Versions of this result can be found in Benzing/Kolonko (1987), Lemma 4.3 and in Milgrom (1981), Proposition 1.

PROOF. *We prove the assertion only for an increasing MLR.*
Let $(n, y), (n', y') \in \mathbf{N}_0 \times \mathbf{R}$ with $(n, y) \leq (n', y')$ and let $D \subseteq \Theta$ be an increasing set. For $\theta' \in D$ and $\theta \in \overline{D} := \Theta \backslash D$ we have $\theta < \theta'$ and therefore

$$\int_D g(n, y; \theta')\overline{\mu}(d\theta')/g(n, y; \theta) \leq \int_D g(n', y'; \theta')\overline{\mu}(d\theta')/g(n', y'; \theta).$$

Having taken the reciprocal we obtain

$$\int_D g(n, y; \theta')\overline{\mu}(d\theta') \cdot \int_{\overline{D}} g(n', y'; \theta)\overline{\mu}(d\theta) \leq \int_D g(n', y'; \theta')\overline{\mu}(d\theta') \cdot \int_{\overline{D}} g(n, y; \theta)\overline{\mu}(d\theta).$$

But this is equivalent to

$$\mu(n, y; D)\ \mu(n', y'; \overline{D}) \leq \mu(n', y'; D)\ \mu(n, y; \overline{D}).$$

From this we immediately have: $\mu(n, y; D) \leq \mu(n', y'; D)$, which proves the assertion.

Thus, the posterior distribution for the unknown parameter θ is a monotone *tp* in the case of the Bernoulli, the Normal, and the Lognormal distribution; for the Gamma distribution the *tp* is antimonotone.

Consequently one step remains to be made in this three-step–process: After having shown that the probability mass function (density function) of the sufficient statistic Y has a monotone likelihood ratio and that the transition probability μ is (anti-)monotone, the same property remains to be shown for the posterior distribution X of the return or the market value that has been defined in (2,5) by the *tp* p.

First of all, we have to investigate the stochastic dominance of the distribution $\nu_\theta(.)$ as a function of θ for the distributions considered in Table 2.1. For these distributions the following statements are well–known (see e.g. Stoyan (1983), pp. 6):

LEMMA 2.12. *Let $B \subseteq \mathcal{X}$ be an increasing set.*
Then $\theta \to \nu_\theta(B)$ is

a) *nondecreasing for the Bernoulli, Normal, and Lognormal distribution,*
b) *nonincreasing for the Gamma distribution.*

We are now in the position to formulate our main result:

THEOREM 2.13. *Let $B \subseteq \mathcal{X}$ be an increasing set and let (n, y) and (n', y') be two information states with $(n, y) \leq (n', y')$ defined in (2,8). Then we have:*

$$p(n, y; B) \leq p(n', y'; B),$$

i.e. p is a monotone transition probability.

PROOF. *Using Lemma 2.11 and Lemma 2.12 the assertion follows immediately from Theorem 2.7 and Corollary 2.8, respectively.*

We conclude this section by drawing the attention to the special case of the Bernoulli distribution once more. In this situation it is possible to compare two information states by means of the more general relation (2,8'): $(n, y) \leq (n', y')$ if and only if $y \leq y'$ and $n - y \geq n' - y'$.

The family of distributions of the sufficient statistic $Y = T(X_1, \ldots, X_n)$, namely the Binomial distributions $b(n, \theta)$, $\theta \in \Theta$, has also an increasing MLR in the information state (n, y). The consequence is that the posterior success probability

$$p(n, y) := p(n, y; \{1\}) \tag{2,10}$$

is a monotone *tp*, too. Here this already known result (see Hengartner/Kalin/ Theodorescu (1981), Lemma 2.4) has been established for any prior distribution just by means of the monotonicity property of the likelihood ratio.
To sum up:

COROLLARY 2.14. *Let ν_θ be the Bernoulli distribution with unknown parameter $\theta \in (0,1)$. Then we have for any prior distribution $\overline{\mu}$ for θ:*

$$p(n,y) \leq p(n',y'),$$

where (n,y), $(n',y') \in \mathbf{N}_0 \times \mathbf{R}$ and $(n,y) \leq (n',y')$ defined in (2,8'), i.e. $y \leq y'$ and $n-y \geq n'-y'$.

2.2.3 Conjugate Prior Distributions

We have shown in the previous section that the posterior distribution p of the market value and the return, respectively, is a monotone transition probability with respect to the information state (n,y). This probability structure allows to derive qualitative properties of the behaviour of the optimal investment policy in subsequent chapters. Because until now we have not specified the prior distribution $\overline{\mu}$ of the unknown parameter θ in detail, we have neglected numerical considerations. The development of an algorithm for the computation of the optimal decisions or at least their determination by means of simulation becomes only possible by the choice of a concrete prior distribution $\overline{\mu}$ (for the selection of a prior distribution see e.g. Berger (1985), chapter 3). From a computational point of view it is of course desirable, if as well the posterior distribution μ for the unknown parameter θ as the posterior distribution p for the random variable X are members of known families of distributions. This should be valid for any sample information, expressed by the information state (n,y).

If the prior distribution $\overline{\mu}$ and the posterior distribution μ of the parameter θ for all (n,y) belong to the same family of distributions, we call this a (natural)conjugate family of distributions. This name expresses the special functional relationship between this family of distributions of the parameter and the family of distributions of the random variable X (see e.g. De Groot (1970), pp. 159).

the type of the prior distribution should not be attributed to a crucial importance for the analysis of the problem. Before the beginning of the planning process the decision–maker himself will best be able to state his attitudes by specifying subjective parameters of the distribution of random variable X besides from objective data from the past. For example, these parameters can be the prior excepted return, the variance of the prior distribution, but one may also think of the mode and therefore the skewness of the distribution. From these quantities it is then possible to compute the "known" parameters of the distribution of X as well as the parameters of the prior distribution, whose type has already been fixed (see for this subject Berger (1985), section 4.7).

After these remarks concerning "statistical practice" we must ask ourselves the question, whether there exist conjugate families of distributions for the distributions considered in Table 2.1. As for these distributions for each sample size n sufficient statistics of constant dimension, namely of dimension one, exist we may conclude the existence of a one-dimensional conjugate family of distributions (see e.g. De Groot (1970), pp. 163, and Lindley (1970), pp. 55).

We explain this fact from the common characterization of the distributions ν_θ as members of a one-parameter exponential family. Let us therefore recapitulate the form of the probability mass function (density function) of the sufficient statistic $Y = T(X_1, \ldots, X_n)$ from (2,9) and (2,3), namely:

$$g(n, y; \theta) = a(\theta)^n H^*(n, y) \exp\left(y b(\theta)\right).$$

Furthermore, in the following we restrict ourselves to continuous prior distributions for θ. We denote the prior density for θ by $\overline{h}$ and the posterior density for θ by h. If the prior density $\overline{h}$ is proportional to $a(\theta)^\gamma \exp\left(\delta b(\theta)\right)$, i.e.

$$\overline{h}(\theta) \propto a(\theta)^\gamma \exp\left(\delta b(\theta)\right), \quad \gamma, \delta \in \mathbf{R}, \tag{2,11}$$

we have for the posterior density h, given the information state (n, y):

$$h(n, y; \theta) \propto a(\theta)^{n+\gamma}\, exp\left((y+\delta) b(\theta)\right).$$

Thus, the prior and the posterior distribution for the unknown parameter θ belong to the same family of distributions. This guarantees for the distributions ν_θ from Table 2.1 that a conjugate prior distribution for θ of the type (2,11) always exists. For three of the four distributions from Table 2.1 the conjugate prior distributions are well known, namely the pairs Binomial–Beta, Gamma–Gamma, and Normal–Normal distribution.

A summary is found in Table 2.2. In the fourth column of that table we also present the type of the posterior distribution p of random variable X.

Table 2.2:
Posterior distributions for information state (n, y)

ν_θ probability distribution	$\overline{\mu}$ prior distribution	μ posterior distribution	p posterior distribution
Bernoulli $b(1,\theta)$	Beta $B(\gamma,\delta)$	$B(\gamma+y,\delta+n-y)$	$b(1,p(n,y))$ $p(n,y) := \frac{\gamma+y}{\gamma+\delta+n}$
Gamma $G(\alpha,\theta)$	Gamma $G(\gamma,\delta)$	$G(\gamma+n\alpha,\delta+y)$	Pearson–Type VI (2.12)
Normal $N(\theta,\sigma^2)$	Normal $N(\mu,\tau^2)$	$N(\mu(n,y),\tau_n^2)$ $\mu(n,y) := \frac{\tau^2 y+\sigma^2\mu}{\tau^2 n+\sigma^2}$	$N(\mu(n,y),\sigma^2+\tau_n^2)$ $\tau_n^2 := \frac{\sigma^2\tau^2}{\tau^2 n+\sigma^2}$
Lognormal $LN(\theta,\sigma^2)$	Normal $N(\mu,\tau^2)$	$N(\mu_\ell(n,y),\tau_n^2)$ $\mu_\ell(n,y) := \frac{\tau^2\log y+\sigma^2\mu}{\tau^2 n+\sigma^2}$	$LN(\mu_\ell(n,y),\sigma^2+\tau_n^2)$

Of separate interest – because less known – is the type of posterior distribution p in the case of a Gamma distributed random variable X and Gamma distributed parameter θ. Suppose we have obtained the information (n, y) and θ is $G(\gamma,\delta)$-Gamma distributed. Then p is the following special Pearson–Type VI-distribution, whose density is denoted by $\overline{p}$ (see Johnson/Kotz (1970), pp. 86):

$$(2{,}12)\quad \overline{p}(n,y;x) = \frac{\Gamma((n+1)\alpha+\gamma)\,(\delta+y)^{n\alpha+\gamma}}{\Gamma(\alpha)\Gamma(n\alpha+\gamma)}\frac{x^{\alpha-1}}{(\delta+y+x)^{(n+1)\alpha+\gamma}}.$$

To the best of our knowledge we have been unable to find a conjugate prior distribution in the literature if ν_θ is the Lognormal distribution. It was no surprise for us to arrive at the Normal distribution as conjugate prior. A proof of this interesting relationship goes along the same lines as in the Normal case, essentially by forming closed quadratic expressions of the variables under consideration.

Now we take this last example of natural conjugate distributions to explain the previously indicated ideas of the actual computation of the parameters of the distributions that are assumed to be "known", in this case σ^2, μ and τ^2.

Suppose at the beginning of the planning process the decision–maker is able to determine the sample mean $\overline{x}$, the sample variance s^2 and the sample skewness γ_1 from past data of the random variable X, say the return of a stock or the market value of an investment perhaps enriched with subjective beliefs. Without loss of generality we start at the beginning of the planning process with information state $(n, y) = (0, 1)$, i.e. we have made no observation and the multiplicative sufficient statistic is one.

Then we have: $\mu_\ell(0,1) = \mu$ and $\tau_0^2 = \tau^2$. Thus, random variable X is initially $LN(\mu, \sigma^2 + \tau^2)$-distributed (see Table 2.2).

The equations for the three considered sample moments are as follows:

$$\begin{aligned}
&\exp(\mu + (\sigma^2 + \tau^2)/2) = \overline{x} \\
&\exp(2\mu + \sigma^2 + \tau^2)[\exp(\sigma^2 + \tau^2) - 1] = s^2 \\
&[\exp(\sigma^2 + \tau^2) - 1]^{1/2}[\exp(\sigma^2 + \tau^2) + 2] = \gamma_1 .
\end{aligned}$$

This system of equations can now be used to compute the "known" parameters σ^2, μ, and τ^2 provided that the sample skewness γ_1 is positive – the Lognormal distribution has positive skewness –, otherwise the decision–maker can stress his risk–averse behaviour by adding a "risk constant" or change to a "risk–taking" distribution, i.e. a distribution with negative skewness.

3. Dynamic Portfolio Models under Uncertainty

It is a world-wide observable phenomenon that one of the most popular financial assets is the regular savings account. The main reason seems to be that it is very liquid. Although savings accounts offer fairly low interest rates, they are often used by individuals and also by small companies (see Brealey/Myers (1981), pp. 619).

The binary portfolio model, analysed in section 3.2, seems to fit perfectly for an individual who has already accumulated a lot of money on his savings account. In the following we call him small investor.

The small investor considers putting part of his savings into a risky asset, say a stock. Furthermore, suppose he has already decided on a certain company. He makes the decision to invest dependent on the stock prices and dividends as well as on his beliefs in the future development of the company and of the whole industry. Once he has invested in the stock, he has to ask the question how long to maintain this commitment. Therefore, he considers his investment activities as an adaptive dynamic process in order to prevent financial losses: in each planning period the probability distribution of the return is updated by means of the actual stock price. But if the rate of return of the stock drops dramatically below the interest rate offered for savings accounts, the small investor is disappointed, sells his stocks and transfers the earned money back to his savings account.

As already mentioned, this described scenario is one possible interpretation of the binary dynamic portfolio model under conditions of uncertainty, presented in section 3.2. There we are dealing with the fundamental question whether to invest in a risky asset (previously the stock) with an a priori only incompletely known distribution of returns or whether to put the money into another risky asset with known return distribution or into a riskless asset (previously the savings account) during a prespecified planning period. That is, we have to decide whether to invest all the money in the one or the other asset. We call this type of investment behaviour "diversification over time".

This is in contrast with the usual definition of diversification, where the investor is faced with the problem to determine how the whole money has to be allocated to the different assets. This classic problem of portfolio selection is addressed to in section 3.1, where a multiperiod model with the aim of maximizing the expected utility of terminal wealth over a given planning horizon is considered. We restrict the attention to the important case of only two assets and focus the analysis first of all on those properties of the optimal portfolio policy that are of interest for the subsequent binary portfolio model.

3.1 Classic Dynamic Portfolio Models

In this section we investigate the so–called classic portfolio model with two assets, where the adjective "classic" only refers to the structure of the investment decisions, namely to the partition (diversification) of the wealth on the assets that are at the investor's disposal.

We assume that asset A is riskless whereas asset B is a risky one. Because we are only considering models in discrete time, the return r_t of asset B in planning period t is defined as the random variable

$$(3,1) \qquad r_t := (P_{t+1} + D_t) \; / \; P_t \; ,$$

where P_t denotes the market price of the asset at the beginning of planning period t, and D_t are the dividend and interest payments, respectively, in period t.

Clearly $r_t - 1$ defines the rate of return of asset B.
If the riskless asset A is a savings account, then its return s describes one plus interest rate.

In the analysis of multiperiod portfolio models in every period the investment decision of an individual usually consists of two parts: the consumption decision and the actual portfolio decision. At the beginning of each planning period the decision–maker determines what is needed for consumption purposes from the initial wealth. The selection of the portfolio then says how the remaining wealth has to be allocated to the different assets (see e.g.Samuelson (1969)). But as has already been mentioned in the introductory remarks of this chapter, the type of investor considered takes his consumption and investment decisions independently because only the optimal partition of the already existing savings is of interest.

Thus, the investor decides in such a way that the expected utility of the final wealth after T planning periods is maximal, where T is the (given) planning horizon.
Denoting the initial wealth of planning period t by x_t and the fraction invested in the risky asset B by u_t, we are confronted with the following optimization problem:

$$(3,2) \qquad \max_{u_1,\ldots,u_T} E\{U(x_{T+1})\}$$

with respect to

$$x_{t+1} = [s(1-u_t) + r_t u_t]\, x_t\,, \quad t = 1,\ldots,T\,, \tag{3,3}$$

where complete reinvestment is assumed.

The von Neumann–Morgenstern utility function U is assumed to be increasing, concave and twice continuously differentiable.

Given the initial wealth x_1, the optimal decisions of the investor crucially depend on his risk preferences. These are expressed by the utility function U but also by the probability distributions of the returns r_t of the risky asset B. Whereas we reserve the latter possibility for the second section, we are now going to discuss measures of risk for utility functions. For independently distributed returns $r_1,\ldots,r_T$ with known distributions we derive for certain classes of utility functions the optimal investment policy by means of stochastic dynamic programming afterwards. Furthermore, some important properties of the optimal investment decisions, like monotonicity, are discussed.

We conclude with some extensions of the basic model just sketched, mainly concerning the assumption which states the independence of the returns of the risky asset B. We are concentrating on such return distributions that depend on an a priori unknown parameter but are independent for given values of the parameter. When we start from a Bayesian point of view, the specification of a prior distribution for the unknown parameter as well as the inclusion of already realized returns of asset B lead in our opinion in a "natural" way to dependent posterior distributions of the returns.

3.1.1. Risk Preferences

The von Neumann–Morgenstern utility U was previously assumed to be increasing and concave. The first property, the monotonicity, is evident, because in any case an investor will value higher wealth with higher utility. The concavity–property means that for every probability distribution of final wealth x_{T+1}, given by the return distribution r_T by means of (3,3), for which $E(x_{T+1})$ and $E(U(x_{T+1}))$ exist, holds:

$$U(E(x_{T+1})) \geq E(U(x_{T+1}))\,. \tag{3,4}$$

This is exactly Jensen's inequality (see e.g. Berger (1985), p. 40).

This is the definition of risk aversion usually employed in statistical decision theory: the investor prefers expected final wealth to random final wealth, a very common behaviour in reality as for example, the large number of insurance contracts indicates.

If the utility function is convex, then in (3,4) as an expression of risk–taking behaviour the reversed inequality sign holds clearly. Consequently, a risk neutral desicion–maker is characterized by an affine utility function; due to the linearity of the expectation operator, in this case the equality sign holds in (3,4).

It is not necessary to express the risk preference, i.e. risk aversion, by means of the utility function itself, but it can also be described by a measure of risk aversion. Here we limit ourselves to the best known of these measures, namely that of Pratt–Arrow (see Pratt (1964), Arrow (1971); for other measures of risk aversion, especially those of Ross and Rubinstein, see e.g. Kallberg/Ziemba (1984)).

The measure of absolute risk aversion in the sense of Pratt/Arrow is defined as

$$A(x) := -U''(x)/U'(x)\,, \tag{3,5}$$

where x denotes final wealth. Due to the assumptions concerning U, the measure A is always nonnegative. Now we know that the von Neumann–Morgenstern utility function U can only be determined up to positive affine transformations. Therefore, utility function U can be reconstructed from measure of absolute risk aversion A, as A is invariant with respect to positive affine transformations. This means that two utility functions U and $\overline{U}$, defined as $\overline{U} := cU + d$, have the same measure of absolute risk aversion, provided that $c > 0$.
Another, although related, measure of risk aversion is the measure of relative (proportional) risk aversion in the sense of Pratt/Arrow:

$$R(x) := -xU''(x)/U'(x) = xA(x)\,. \tag{3,6}$$

Empirical studies showed that it is plausible to assume nonincreasing absolute risk aversion A and nondecreasing relative risk aversion (see e.g. Kischka (1984), pp. 28 and Tesfatsion (1981), pp. 66). Later we will return to this point and argue that these properties represent not only empirically but also theoretically sensible behavioural assumptions.

For matter of presentation sometimes the reciprocal of the measure of absolute risk aversion is used; it is defined as risk–tolerance function A^{-1}.

In dynamic portfolio theory mainly utility functions with affine risk–tolerance function are considered, i.e.

$$A^{-1}(x) = a + bx \,, \tag{3,7}$$

where the real numbers a and b specify the parameters of the utility function U. From the desired properties of the measures of risk aversion, namely $A' \leq 0$ and $R' \geq 0$, we immediately conclude that the parameters a and b have to be nonnegative real numbers, i.e. $a, b \geq 0$.

The importance of (3,7) for dynamic portfolio models lies in the possibility of determining closed form solutions of the optimal investment decisions of each period. This will be demonstrated in detail in the next subsection.

The following forms of utility functions have an affine risk–tolerance function (3,7):

(3,8) a) exponential: $$U(x) = -e^{-x/a} \quad \text{for} \quad b = 0 \,,$$

(3,9) b) logarithmic: $$U(x) = \log(x + a) \quad \text{for} \quad b = 1 \,,$$

(3,10) c) power: $$U(x) = \frac{1}{b-1}(a + bx)^{1-\frac{1}{b}} \quad \text{otherwise} \,.$$

Two important special cases can be deduced directly:

1) Exponential utility functions (3,8) have constant absolute risk aversion, i.e. $A(x) = 1/a$.
2) Logarithmic and power utility functions (3,9) and (3,10), respectively, have constant relative risk aversion, i.e. $R(x) = 1/b$, provided that parameter $a = 0$.

Until now we have discussed the risk attitudes of investors with respect to the utility function U. Next we briefly turn towards the risk preferences expressed by the distributions of final wealth x_{T+1}, which are induced by different investment policies. It is no surprise that this leads us to the field of stochastic monotonicity (dominance).

The optimality criterion (3,2) together with (3,3) determines the optimal investment policy by means of the Bernoulli principle, i.e. it maximizes the expected utility of final wealth.

In the following instead of x_{T+1} we write simply x for the final wealth. Let now two investment policies $u^1 := (u_1^1, \ldots, u_T^1)$ and $u^2 := (u_1^2, \ldots, u_T^2)$ be given and let x^1 and x^2 be the induced final wealths. According to the Bernoulli principle u^1 is preferred to u^2 if and only if

$$E(U(x^1)) > E(U(x^2)).$$

In the terminology of Rothschild/Stiglitz (1970) final wealth x^1 is "less risky" than final wealth x^2.

Let F_1 (F_2) be the distribution function of $x^1(x^2)$. Then the following holds:

THEOREM 3.1. *The following statements are equivalent:*

a) $\int_{-\infty}^{x} F_1(t)\,dt \le \int_{-\infty}^{x} F_2(t)\,dt$.

b) *For all nondecreasing, concave functions U holds:*

$$E(U(x^1)) \ge E(U(x^2)),$$

provided that the expected values exist.

c) *There exists a random variable z such that x^2 and $x^1 + z$ have the same distribution, and the conditional expectation $E(z|x^1) \le 0$ with probability one.*

Moreover, if x^1 and x^2 have the same expected value, then the statements of Theorem 3.1 are equivalent for concave functions U in b) and $E(z|x^1) = 0$ in c).

For the equivalence of a) and b) see Stoyan (1983), Theorem 1.4.1, for the equivalence of b) and c) see Brumelle/Vickson (1975), Theorem 3.2.

Statement a) is the usual definition of second order stochastic dominance (Stoyan (1983), pp. 11), in contrast to the better known (first order) stochastic dominance which is defined by $F_1(x) \le F_2(x)$, i.e. random variable x^1 takes on higher values with higher probability than random variable x^2.

Statement c) means that random variable x^2 has the same distribution as x^1 plus the noise–term z. We explain this by an example: The two random final wealths x^1 and x^2 are normally distributed with common expected value μ: $x^1 \sim N(\mu, \sigma_1^2)$, $x^2 \sim N(\mu, \sigma_2^2)$. As can be checked easily, statement b) is fulfilled if $\sigma_1 \le \sigma_2$. Thus, x^1 is less risky than x^2, where the smaller risk of x^1 is only expressed by the smaller variance σ_1^2.

But we want to warn against a generalization of the statement that smaller risk is equivalent to smaller variance. Let for example the final wealth x^i be $G(\alpha_i, \theta_i)$–Gamma distributed, $i = 1, 2$, then x^2 is less risky than x^1 in the sense of (first order) stochastic dominance if $\alpha_1 \leq \alpha_2$ and $\theta_1 \geq \theta_2$. This means that $E(x^1) \leq E(x^2)$ and $\text{Var}(x^1) \leq \text{Var}(x^2)$. Now we know that (first order) stochastic dominance implies second order stochastic dominance. In the terminology of Rothschild/Stiglitz therefore in this case the final wealth x^2 is in spite of larger variance, but also larger expected value, less risky than final wealth x^1.

The result: Second order stochastic dominance, represented by Theorem 3.1, is a more comprehensive criterion than the mean–variance principle.

3.1.2. Classic Dynamic Portfolio Models under Risk

In this section we discuss the classic dynamic portfolio model under conditions of risk, i.e. the distribution of the return of the risky asset B is known for all periods at the beginning of the planning process. We begin with presenting the basic assumptions in detail. Then the model is formulated as a stochastic dynamic program, the optimal investment policy is determined and its basic properties are derived. Finally we survey the literature concerning generalizations of the basic model.

3.1.2.1. Assumptions

With a view to greater clarity we put together the assumptions of the model that have already been mentioned in part:

A1. There are no transaction costs and no taxes. The two assets considered are completely divisible.

A2. The aim of the investor is the maximization of the expected utility of the final wealth x_{T+1} for T planning periods, where T is the given planning horizon (cp. (3,2)).
The increasing concave utility function U has an affine risk–tolerance function

$$A^{-1}(x_{T+1}) = a + bx_{T+1} \quad \text{for} \quad a, b \geq 0.$$

Consumption decisions are not taken into consideration.

A3. The return of the riskless asset A is constant over time; it is denoted by s. The returns of the risky asset $B, r_1, \ldots, r_T$ are *iid* random variables. Therefore, we write for the return simply r. Complete reinvestment of the initial wealth x_t in planning period t leads to the following transformation equation for wealth (cp. (3.3)):

$$x_{t+1} = [(1 - u_t)s + u_t r]\, x_t \ , \quad t = 1, \ldots, T$$

where u_t represents the proportion of the initial wealth x_t that is invested in the risky asset B.

On the one hand, A3 is a stationarity–assumption: the same return for A and the same return distribution for B in all planning periods. Besides from the otherwise occuring problem of obtaining all the necessary information, this is only done to ease notation.

On the other hand, the assumption of independence of the returns of B means an essential restriction. In this way it is indirectly expressed that the investor acts as a "price taker". He does not assume that his investment decisions have an effect on the distribution of the return of the risky asset B; in planning period t the proportion u_t uniquely determines by means of transformation equation (3,3) the distribution of final wealth x_{t+1}. In any case this seems to be suitable for the assumed small investor.

But the postulate of the independence of the returns over time is the starting point for further portfolio models which will be discussed briefly after the analysis of the basic model.

A4. The "no–easy–money–condition" holds: Realizations of the random return r of asset B which are smaller than the riskless return s of asset A, i.e. $P(r < s) > 0$, exist (cp. Hakansson (1970), p. 589) . This assumption assures together with

$$\lim_{x \to \infty} U'(x) = 0 \quad \text{and} \quad \lim_{x \to -\infty} U'(x) > 0 \tag{3,11}$$

that the set of possible proportions u_t is a compact subinterval of $\mathbf{R}$ for all initial wealths $x_t, t = 1, \ldots, T$ (cp. Bertsekas (1974), Proposition 5).

If this assumption is violated, the investor will tend to put as much as possible into the risky asset B by borrowing the necessary amount of money at the riskless rate $s - 1$; or the other way round: The investor will put as much as possible money into asset A at the riskless return s by selling short the necessary amount of the risky asset B, i.e. $u_t < 0$.

Property (3,11) is fullfilled for the utility functions specified by (3,8) —(3,10), as we assumed parameters a and b to be nonnegative.

A5. The expected return of the risky asset B is not smaller than the riskless return s of asset A, i.e. $E(r) \geq s$.

As will be shown later, this assumption guarantees that it is never optimal to sell short the risky asset B, i.e. that always $u_t \geq 0$, $t = 1, \ldots, T$, holds.

3.1.2.2. The Optimal Investment Policy and its Properties

For the determination and the characterization of the optimal investment decisions it is reasonable to formulate the portfolio model as a stochastic dynamic program. Pioneer work in this direction has been carried out by Mossin (1968), Samuelson (1969) and Hakansson (1970); an excellent summary is contained in Bertsekas (1976), pp. 89.

Because our objective is just the maximization of the expected utility of terminal wealth at the planning horizon T, discounting clearly does not matter. Furthermore, at the moment we place no restrictions on the investment decisions, for example we allow for short sales of the risky asset B.

The stochastic dynamic program with finite planning horizon T therefore is given by the tupel (X, K, D, p, w, U) of the following meaning:

a) the state space $X := \mathbf{R}^+ := [0, \infty)$; $x \in X$ denotes the initial wealth of a planning period,
b) the control (action) space $K := \mathbf{R}$; $u \in K$ is the proportion of x that is invested in the risky asset B,
c) the disturbance space $D := \mathbf{R}$; $r \in D$ is the (random) return of asset B, defined in (3,1),
d) the disturbance distribution p specifies the probability distribution of return r,
e) the state transition function $w : X \times K \times D \to X$ of the initial wealth in each planning period, defined in (3,3), i.e.

$$x_{t+1} = w(x_t, u, r) = [(1-u)s + ur]x_t \ ,$$

f) the final reward function $U : X \to \mathbf{R}$, where $U(x)$ represents the utility of the final wealth at the end of planning period T.
U is given by (3,8)—(3,10).

The no–easy–money–condition (assumption A4) guarantees that the control space is a closed subinterval of $\mathbf{R}$. Together with the functional form of the state transition w this means that the utility function is bounded above. Thus, all properties of the so–called semicontinuous dynamic program are satisfied with the consequence that an optimal (deterministic) Markov policy exists (cp. Bertsekas/Shreve (1978), pp. 208).

The value functions of dynamic programming $\mathcal{J}_t : X \to \mathbf{R}$ are therefore well defined. $\mathcal{J}_t(x)$ denotes the optimal expected (indirect) utility from planning period t to the planning horizon $T+1$, when the initial wealth in period t is x. These value or indirect utility functions $\mathcal{J}_t$ are determined recursively by means of the value iteration procedure of dynamic programming (cp. e.g. Bertsekas/Shreve (1978), chapter 8):

$$\begin{aligned} \mathcal{J}_{T+1}(x) &= U(x) \\ \overline{\mathcal{J}}_t(x,u) &= \int \mathcal{J}_{t+1}([(1-u)s+ur]x)\,p(dr) \\ &= E\{\mathcal{J}_{t+1}([(1-u)s+ur]x)\} \\ \mathcal{J}_t(x) &= \max_{u\in K} \overline{\mathcal{J}}_t(x,u)\,, \quad 1 \le t \le T\,. \end{aligned} \tag{3,12}$$

For $1 \le t \le T$ and $x \in X$ the optimal investment policy is a finite sequence $(f_1,\dots,f_T)$ of functions $f_t : X \to K$ determined by

$$\mathcal{J}_t(x) = \overline{\mathcal{J}}_t(x, f_t(x))\,. \tag{3,13}$$

The optimal investment decision (function) $f_t(x)$ specifies that proportion of the initial wealth x which in period t has to be invested in the risky asset B.

Remember that assumption A2 states that the utility function U has an affine risk–tolerance function. In the following we show that the same property is valid for the value functions $\mathcal{J}_t$, $1 \le t \le T$, whereas the optimal investment decisions are affine in the reciprocal of the initial wealth of a planning period.

THEOREM 3.2. *Suppose the utility function U has an affine risk–tolerance function $A^{-1}(x) = a + bx$. Then for $1 \le t \le T$ we have:*

a) $f_t(x) = c_t[a/(xs^{T-t}) + bs]$,
where parameters c_t are determined from the distribution p of the random return r of the risky asset B.

b) $-\mathcal{J}_t'(x)/\mathcal{J}_t''(x) = a/s^{T-t+1} + bx$.

PROOF. *By simultaneous backward induction over a) and b) starting with $t = T$.*

a) *Suppose parameter c_T depends on the initial wealth x in period T:*

$$f_T(x) = c_T(x)(a/x + bs)\,.$$

Now define the corresponding final wealth in period T by $\overline{x}$, i.e.

$$\overline{x} := sx - (r+s)c_T(x)(a+bsx)\,.$$

Then from the necessary optimality condition we have:

$$E\{U'(\overline{x})(r-s)\} = 0\,.$$

Differentiation with respect to x yields:

$$E\{U''(\overline{x})(r-s)[s+(r-s)c'_T(x)(a+bsx)+(r-s)c_T(x)bs]\} = 0\,. \tag{3,14}$$

The risk–tolerance function for the terminal wealth $\overline{x}$ can be written in the following way:

$$A^{-1}(\overline{x}) = -U'(\overline{x})/U''(\overline{x}) = a + b\overline{x} = (a+bsx)[1+(r-s)c_T(x)b]\,. \tag{3,15}$$

By inserting in (3,14) we obtain:

$$\begin{aligned} -E\{U'(\overline{x})(r-s)^2/[1+(r-s)c_T(x)b]\}c'_T(x) \\ = E\{U'(\overline{x})(r-s)\}s/(a+bsx)\,. \end{aligned}$$

The right hand side of this equation is zero due to the optimality condition, and the expectation on the left hand side of the equation is not equal to zero in general. Thus, $c'_T(x)$ must be zero, which means that $c_T(x)$ is a constant.

b) *We have*

$$\mathcal{J}_T(x) = E\{U(\overline{x})\} = E\{U(s[1+(r-s)c_Tb]x + (r-s)c_Ta)\}\,.$$

Then

$$\mathcal{J}'_T(x) = E\{U'(\overline{x})s[1+(r-s)c_Tb]\}$$

and

$$\mathcal{J}''_T(x) = E\{U''(\overline{x})s^2[1+(r-s)c_Tb]^2\}\,.$$

Using (3,15) we obtain

$$\mathcal{J}''_T(x) = -E\{U'(\overline{x})s[1+(r-s)c_Tb]\}s/(a+bsx)$$

and therefore

$$-\mathcal{J}'_T(x)/\mathcal{J}''_T(x) = a/s + bx\,.$$

The general step of the proof by backward induction is shown in the same manner as the one just demonstrated for the beginning of the induction.

The importance of the exponential, logarithmic and power utility functions defined in (3,8)–(3,10) is illustrated by property b) of the preceding theorem in an impressive way. The structure of the measures of risk aversion of the dynamic model's value functions $\mathcal{J}_t$ is the same as that of the utility function U itself. For $A(x) = (a + bx)^{-1}$ the measure of absolute risk aversion for $\mathcal{J}_t$ is equal to $(a/s^{T-t+1} + bx)^{-1}$. This allows a possible interpretation of parameter a of the utility function U. It can be looked at as deterministic income a at the planning horizon T. Then parameter $a_t := a/s^{T-t+1}$ of the indirect utility function $\mathcal{J}_t$ represents the present value of this income in period t, discounted with the return of the riskless asset A.

Furthermore, we have mentioned that absolute risk aversion $A(x)$ is nonincreasing and relative risk aversion $R(x)$ is nondecreasing in initial wealth x if the parameters a and b of utility U are nonnegative. It can easily be seen that these properties remain valid for the risk aversion measures of the indirect utility functions $\mathcal{J}_t$, $1 \leq t \leq T$. This is also proved for a more general dynamic investment model in Tesfatsion (1981), Theorem 3.3.

Now we turn the attention to statement a) of Theroem 3.2, namely the optimal proportion $f_t(x)$ that in period t has to be invested in the risky asset B, given initial wealth x. A direct consequence is

COROLLARY 3.3.

a) *Let the measure of absolute risk aversion be constant, i.e.* $A(x) = 1/a$ *for* $b = 0$. *Then in each planning period* t *the optimal part of the initial wealth* x *that is invested in the risky asset* B *is constant, i.e.* $xf_t(x) = c_t a/s^{T-t}$, $1 \leq t \leq T$.
b) *Let the measure of relative risk aversion be constant, i.e.* $R(x) = 1/b$ *for* $a = 0$. *Then in each planning period* t *the optimal fraction of the initial wealth* x *that is invested in the risky asset* B *is constant, i.e.* $f_t(x) = c_t bs$, $1 \leq t \leq T$.

Part a) of the corollary says that an investor with exponential utility function of final wealth (3,8) in each planning period t puts the amount $c_t\, a/s^{T-t}$ into the risky asset B, which is independent of the respective initial wealth. This amount is composed of the present value of income a at the planning horizon and a "risk constant" c_t, which is determined by the return distribution of asset B. If, for example, the return of B is a $N(\mu, \sigma^2)$–Normal distribution, the optimal amount which in period t has to be invested in B is given by $(\mu - s)/\sigma^2 \, a/s^{T-t}$. Thus, the risk constant is the ratio of expected excess return $(\mu - s)$ and the variance of the return σ^2. We immediately can see from this form of c_t that it is only optimal to invest in B if the expected return μ of B is larger than the return s of the riskless asset A. Furthermore, greater risk, in this case only represented by the variance σ^2 , leads to a decrease of the amount invested in the risky asset B.

From part b) of the above corollary we conclude the constancy of the optimal proportion invested in B in each period, provided that the investor has a logarithmic (3,9) or power (3,10) utility function of final wealth whose measure of relative risk aversion is also constant, i.e. $a = 0$. This property is of great importance for the binary portfolio model. Decreasing risk aversion, expressed by a larger value of parameter b, leads to an increase of the optimal proportion $c_t \, bs$ in period t. This optimal amount can be interpreted as the risk–weighted value at time $t+1$ of one monetary unit put into the riskless asset with return s at time t. The investor's risk attitudes are represented by parameter b of utility function U and again by the risk constant c_t of the distribution of the return of asset B.

The preceding remarks make it clear that the investor acts in this situation as a single–period decision–maker, because he does not look beyond the end of the actual planning period in order to determine the optimal portfolio decision. The investor does not take into account the possibility of reinvesting his wealth in subsequent planning periods. This aspect is expressed in the general investment decision by the term $a/(xs^{T-t})$ (cp. Theorem 3.2. a)).

In summary: Constant relative risk aversion of the utility function of final wealth implies not only the independence of the optimal proportion $f_t(x)$ invested in the risky asset B of the initial wealth in each period t but also the optimality of a myopic investment decision.

In the following we investigate the monotonic behaviour of the optimal investment decision functions $f_t(x)$, $1 \le t \le T$, from Theorem 3.2.a). We state reasonable properties guaranteeing the optimal proportion $f_t(x)$ to be nonincreasing in initial wealth x. Because the utility function of final wealth U is assumed to be increasing and concave, we have the following well–known result which is a direct consequence of Theorem 3.2.b).

LEMMA 3.4. *For $1 \le t \le T$ the value functions of dynamic programming $\mathcal{J}_t$, defined in* (3,12)*, are increasing and concave.*

The proof goes by backward induction and can be found e.g. in Kischka (1984), pp. 102.

Now recall assumption A5; it states that the expected return $E(r)$ of asset B is not smaller than the riskless return s of asset A. We show that by this assumption short sales of the risky asset B are excluded.

LEMMA 3.5.

a) *The expected return of asset B is equal to the riskless return s of asset A, i.e. $E(r) = s$, if and only if in each planning period t all the initial wealth x is invested in the riskless asset A, i.e. $f_t(x) = 0$, $1 \le t \le T$.*

b) *The expected return of asset B is larger than the riskless return s of asset A, i.e. $E(r) > s$, if and only if in each planning period t at least part of the initial wealth x is invested in the risky asset B, i.e. $f_t(x) > 0$, $1 \le t \le T$.*

PROOF. *For $1 \le t \le T$, let $\overline{x} := [s + (r - s)f_t(x)]\, x$ be the final wealth in planning period t, given the initial wealth x and the optimal investment decision $f_t(x)$. Clearly we have*

$$E\{\mathcal{J}'_{t+1}(\overline{x})(r - s)\} = 0\,. \tag{3,16}$$

a) *Let $E(r) = s$. The necessary optimality condition is satisfied if $f_t(x) = 0$.*
Now if in contrast $f_t(x) = 0$ is optimal, then we have for equation (3,16):

$$\mathcal{J}'_{t+1}(sx)[E(r) - s] = 0\,.$$

By Lemma 3.4, $\mathcal{J}_{t+1}$ is increasing, therefore $E(r) = s$ must hold. This proof is the same as the one for the single–period model (cp. Merton (1982), Theorem 2.2).

b) *Because $f_t(x)$ is optimal, we have on the one hand:*

$$E\{\mathcal{J}_{t+1}(\overline{x})\} > E\{\mathcal{J}_{t+1}(sx)\} = \mathcal{J}_{t+1}(sx)\,.$$

One the other hand, we obtain from the concavity of $\mathcal{J}_{t+1}$ (Lemma 3.4) using Jensen's inequality:

$$E\{\mathcal{J}_{t+1}(\overline{x})\} \le \mathcal{J}_{t+1}([s + (E(r) - s)\, f_t(x)]x)$$

The monotonicity of $\mathcal{J}_{t+1}$ means that

$$[E(r) - s]\, f_t(x) > 0\,.$$

Now the assertion can be simply read off from this inequality.

For one–period portfolio models the following result can be found in Merton (1982), pp. 611:

THEOREM 3.6. *Let the expected return of asset B not be smaller than the riskless return of asset A; i.e. $E(r) > s$.*

Furthermore, let the measure of relative risk aversion of the utility function U as well as the value functions $\mathcal{J}_t$, $1 \le t \le T$, be nondecreasing.

Then the optimal investment decision functions f_t are nonincreasing, i.e. $f_t' \le 0$, $1 \le t \le T$.

PROOF. *As in the proof of Lemma 3.5 we define $\overline{x} := [s + (r - s)\, f_t(x)]\, x$. Then in planning period t the necessary optimality condition is given by:*

$$E\{\mathcal{J}_{t+1}'(\overline{x})(r - s)\} = 0\,.$$

Differentiation with respect to initial wealth x leads to

$$E\{\mathcal{J}_{t+1}''(\overline{x})(r - s)^2\, x\}\, f_t'(x) = -E\{\mathcal{J}_{t+1}''(\overline{x})(r - s)\, \overline{x}/x\}\,.$$

Denoting the measure of relative risk aversion for $\mathcal{J}_{t+1}$ by R we have from (3,6)*:*

$$-\overline{x}\mathcal{J}_{t+1}''(\overline{x}) = R(\overline{x})\mathcal{J}_{t+1}'(\overline{x})$$

and therefore:

$$f_t'(x) = E\{R(\overline{x})\mathcal{J}_{t+1}'(\overline{x})(r - s)\}/[x^2 E\{\mathcal{J}_{t+1}''(\overline{x})(r - s)^2\}]\,.$$

The mean value theorem of differential calculus says that for any $\overline{x}$ there always exists a $\lambda = \lambda(\overline{x})$, $0 \le \lambda \le 1$, such that

$$R(\overline{x}) = R(sx) + R'(\eta)(\overline{x} - sx)\;,$$

where $\overline{\eta} := sx + \lambda(\overline{x} - sx)$.
Thus we have

$$f_t'(x) = [R(sx)E\{\mathcal{J}_{t+1}'(\overline{x})(r - s)\} + E\{R'(\eta)\mathcal{J}_{t+1}'(\overline{x})(r - s)^2\}f_t(x)\, x]$$
$$/[x^2 E\{\mathcal{J}_{t+1}''(\overline{x})(r - s)^2\}]\,.$$

The first expression of the numerator is the necessary optimality condition and is therefore equal to zero. As the denominator is always negative and $\mathcal{J}_{t+1}$ is increasing, the sign of f_t' depends only on $R' \cdot f_t$. By assumption and using Lemma 3.5 this product is nonnegative. Therefore, the optimal investment decision $f_t(x)$ is a nonincreasing function of x.

This result is valid for a larger class of utility functions than those defined in (3,8)–(3,10). For the latter ones the statement of the preceding theorem is evident: By Lemma 3.5 $f_t(x) \geq 0$ holds. Because the parameters a and b of the utility function are nonnegative real numbers, it follows from Theorem 3.2. a) that parameter c_t also must be nonnegative. A direct consequence is the typical behaviour of risk averse investors: The higher the initial wealth of a planning period, the lower is the (relative) proportion invested in the risky asset B. But this plausible behaviour only holds in the situation considered here, i.e. two assets, one of them might be risky.

One of the assumptions of Theorem 3.6 is that the measure of relative risk aversion $R(x)$ is nondecreasing. This clearly raises the question whether there exists a similar result for the measure of absolute risk aversion $A(x)$. The answer is yes (cp. Tesfatsion (1981), Theorem 3.4):

If $E(r) \geq s$ and $A(x)$ are nonincreasing, then the optimal amount invested in the risky asset B is nondecreasing, i.e. $(x\, f_t(x))' \geq 0, 1 \leq t \leq T$. In this situation it is enough to assume the measure of absolute risk aversion of utility function U to be nonincreasing. The same property then follows for the value functions $\mathcal{J}_t$, $1 \leq t \leq T$.

We already mentioned for the case of constant relative risk aversion, i.e. for the utility functions (3,9) and (3,10) with $a = 0$, that decreasing risk aversion, represented by the increasing parameter b, leads to higher optimal proportions invested in the risky asset B.

In the following we briefly discuss the relationship of utility functions (3,8)–(3,10) with respect to the measures of risk aversion. Because parameters a and b are nonnegative by assumption, decreasing risk aversion is achieved by increasing parameter b for constant positive wealth x, as $A(x) = (a+bx)^{-1}$. From Theorem 3.2a) we conclude that the optimal proportions invested in the risky asset B $f_t(x) = c_t[a/(xs^{T-t}) + bs]$ becomes larger, too.

Varying parameter b of the power utility function (3,10), we identify the following limiting cases in the sense of the measure of absolute risk aversion $A(x)$:

a) $\lim_{b\to\infty} A(x) = 0$: Linear utility function (risk neutrality)
b) $\lim_{b\to 1} A(x) = (a+x)^{-1}$: Logarithmic utility function (3,9)
c) $\lim_{b\to 0} A(x) = a^{-1}$: Exponential utility function (3,8)

This shows that from the three classes of utility functions (3,8)– (3,10), the exponential utility function is that one with the largest risk aversion. The logarithmic utility function corresponds to the power utility function with $b = 1$ in the sense of absolute risk aversion.

Thus, an exponential investor puts less money into the risky asset B than the logarithmic one. And an investor with logarithmic utility function, however, puts less money into the risky asset B than the risk–neutral one. We will return to the latter point during the sensitivity analysis of the binary portfolio model.

3.1.2.3 Extended Versions of the Basic Model

The main drawback of the previously introduced dynamic portfolio model is the independence and stationarity of the returns $r_1, \ldots, r_T$ of the risky asset B (cp. assumption A3). Therewith the investor is not allowed to adapt this return distribution to the changing environment of the market by the use of new information obtained during the planning process. But if we instead assume that the investor informs himself regularly and that he possibly revises his preferences and also the future portfolio decisions, we have to ask the crucial question: What sort of information is decisive for the composition of the optimal portfolio ? But much ambiguity exists about the answer to this question and also about the way how investors actually become informed (cp. for this Jennings/Barry (1983)).

It is therefore not surprising that many authors denote these periodical information just as "state of the economy" which influences the return (not only) of the risky assets (cp. e.g. Fama (1970), Hakansson (1971), Merton (1982)). Before specifying in detail this state of the economy, for example as past returns or as security prices, we again represent the extended model as dynamic program, and that by the tupel $(X \times Z, K, D, p, w, \overline{v}, U)$. In the following we only describe those elements of the model which are new and defined in a new way, respectively:

a) $Z := \mathbf{R}^m$; $z \in Z$ is the state of the economy at the beginning of a planning period.
b) the disturbance distribution p is a transition probability from Z to D. It describes the probability distribution of return r depending

on the state of the economy.

c) the transformation of the state of the economy $\overline{v} : Z \times D \to Z$. Given state $z \in Z$ and return $r \in D$ of the risky asset B in a planning period, $\overline{v}(z,r)$ represents the state of the economy in the subsequent planning period.

In order to guarantee the existence of an optimal (deterministic) investment policy, the no–easy–money–condition (assumption A4) has to be satisfied for all states of the economy z, i.e.

$$\int_{-\infty}^{s} p(z; dr) > 0 \quad \text{for all} \quad z \in Z .$$

Assumption A5 has to be extended to rule out short sales of the risky asset B: In each state of the economy the expected return of asset B must not be less than the return of the riskless asset A:

$$E(r|z) := \int rp(z; dr) \geq s \quad \text{for all} \quad z \in Z .$$

To satisfy all assumptions of the semicontinuous dynamic program (cp. Bertsekes/Shreve (1978), pp. 208) the transition probability p has to be continuous. The tpp is said to be continuous, if for all functions g, whose integral with respect to p exist, holds:

$$\int g(r)p(z_n; dr) \to \int g(r)p(z; dr) , \quad \text{if} \quad z_n \to z$$

(cp. e.g. Hinderer (1970),pp. 115).

Therefore, the value functions $\mathcal{J}_t : X \times Z \to \mathbf{R}$, $1 \leq t \leq T+1$, are well–defined. $\mathcal{J}_t(x,z)$ denotes the maximal expected utility from planning period t to the planning horizon $T+1$, when we have wealth x and state of the economy z at the beginning of period t. The value iteration of dynamic programming is of the following form:

$$\mathcal{J}_{T+1}(x,z) = U(x) ,$$

i.e. the utility of terminal wealth is not influenced by the state of the economy z,

$$\overline{\mathcal{J}}_t(x,z,u) = \int \mathcal{J}_{t+1}([(1-u)s + ur]x \, , \overline{v}(z,r))p(z; dr)$$

$$\mathcal{J}_t(x,z) = \max_{u \in K} \overline{\mathcal{J}}_t(x,z,u) , \quad 1 \leq t \leq T . \tag{3,17}$$

For $1 \leq t \leq T$ the optimal investment decision function $f_t(x, z)$ is determined by

$$(3,18) \qquad \mathcal{J}_t(x, z) = \overline{\mathcal{J}}_t(x, z, f_t(x, z)).$$

$f_t(x, z)$ is the proportion of the initial wealth x, which in planning period t is invested in the risky asset B provided the state of the economy is z. As usual, the finite sequence $(f_1, \ldots, f_T)$ constitutes the optimal portfolio policy.

A comparison of (3,18) with the optimal investment decisions of the basic model (3,13) clearly shows the influence of the information represented by the state of the economy z on the optimal portfolio decision $f_t(x, z)$. From the point of view of the dynamic programming model this is achieved by enlarging the state space. In the basic model the state x is one–dimensional, whereas in the extended version the state (x, z) is $(m + 1)$–dimensional, as we assume in a) the state of the economy to be characterized by an m–dimensional vector.

Thus, we are confronted with a fact that Bellman called the "curse of dimensionality" of the state space. From a practical point of view this means that it is nearly impossible to compute the optimal investment decisions numerically.

A first possibility of avoiding this dilemma is to look for conditions that guarantee the optimality of myopic investment decisions. In the basic model this is true for the so–called isoelastic utility functions, i.e. (3,9) and (3,10) with parameter $a = 0$. Now the question arises whether this property of the optimal portfolio policy carries over to the extended model. The answer is in part positive (cp. Hakansson (1971), pp. 330):

In general, the optimal investment decisions are not myopic in the case of a power utility function (3,10) with $a = 0$.

But in the case of the logarithmic utility function $\log x$, i.e. (3,9) with $a = 0$, the optimal investment policy is also myopic, if the return depends on the state of the economy.

This is another substantial reason for the special importance of the logarithmic utility function $\log x$ in the theory of multiperiod portfolio models. This feature as well as the outstanding position of the isoelastic utility functions in general are discussed in detail by Hakansson (1979).

Another possibility to avoid the previously indicated numerical dilemma is the specification of the states of the economy and in agreement with that to reduce their dimension and their quantity, respectively.

It is obvious to fix in planning period t the state of the economy z as return of the risky asset B of the foregoing period $t-1$. In this case the transition of the state of the economy is given by $\overline{v}(z,r) = r$, i.e. the returns of the risky asset B constitute a Markov process.

Miller (1978) defines in planning period t the state of the economy z as the price of the risky asset B at the beginning of period t. The return of B in planning period t is given as a function of its price z and is denoted by $r(z)$. Then the asset price at the beginning of period $t+1$ is $\overline{v}(z,r) = r(z)z$. E.g. in the case that asset B is a stock we assume no dividend–payments during planning period t.

The disturbance distribution is defined in the following way:

$$p(z;E) := P\left(\{w|r(z)(w) \in E\}\right) \ , \ E \subseteq D \,, z \in Z \,.$$

Then the value functions $\overline{\mathcal{J}}_t$ are given by:

$$(3,19) \quad \overline{\mathcal{J}}_t(x,z,u) = \int \mathcal{J}_{t+1}\left([(1-u)s + ur]x, rz\right) p(z;dr)\,, \quad 1 \leq t \leq T\,.$$

It is clearly of interest to investigate under what conditions the optimal proportions invested in asset B $f_t(x,z)$, $1 \leq t \leq T$, are monotone functions of the price z. Obviously a promising approach is the monotonicity–behaviour of the return $r(z)$ as a function of the price z.

Let r be a nondecreasing (nonincreasing) function of z. Then we have for all nondecreasing functions g which are integrabel with respect to p for $z_1 \leq z_2$:

$$\begin{aligned}\int g(r)p(z_1;dr) &= \int g(r(z_1))(w)P(dw) \leq \int g(r(z_2))(w)P(dw)\\ &= \int g(r)p(z_2;dr)\,,\end{aligned}$$

that is, the disturbance distribution is a monotone (antimonotone) transition probability. The value functions of dynamic programming given by (3,17) are then nondecreasing in initial wealth x and additionally nondecreasing (nonincreasing) functions of the asset price z.

In Theorem 3.2a) we have seen that for the utility functions (3,8)– (3,10) the optimal proportion $f_t(x)$ invested in the risky asset B is nonincreasing in initial wealth x. The same holds true for these utility functions also in the generalized model for the optimal investment decisions $f_t(x,z)$ if the price z of asset B is kept constant.

But the investigation of the monotonicity of $f_t(x,z)$ with respect to z keeping initial wealth x constant causes difficulties that we only overcome in the case of the logarithmic utility function $\log x$, which once more underlines its outstanding position. Its evidence is based on a general theorem dealing with the monotonicity of optimal control policies of dynamic programs (Serfozo (1976), Theorem 3.1), adapted to our model:

LEMMA 3.7. *For $1 \le t \le T$ and for all $x \in X$ the optimal decision function $f_t(x,z)$ of the dynamic program defined in* (3,17) *and* (3,18) *is nondecreasing (nonincreasing) in z, if*

$$\overline{\mathcal{J}}_t(x,z,u_2) - \overline{\mathcal{J}}_t(x,z,u_1)$$

is a nondecreasing (nonincreasing) function of z for all $u_1, u_2 \in K$ with $u_1 \le u_2$.

If $U(x) = \log x$, we have for the portfolio model given by the value functions (3,19):

$$\overline{\mathcal{J}}_t(x,z,u) = \log x + \overline{V}_t(z,u) \ ,$$
$$\mathcal{J}_t(x,z) = \log x + V_t(z) \ , \quad 1 \le t \le T \, ,$$

where

$$V_{T+1}(z) \equiv 0$$

and

$$\overline{V}_t(z,u) = [\log((1-u)s + ur) + V_{t+1}(rz)]p(z;dr)$$
$$V_t(z) = \max_{u \in K}\{\overline{V}_t(z,u)\} \ , \quad 1 \le t \le T \, .$$

This relationship can be proved easily by backward induction. Thus, it is enough to investigate the functions $\overline{V}_t(z,u_2) - \overline{V}_t(z,u_1)$ for $u_1 \le u_2$.

We have

$$\overline{V}_t(z,u_2) - \overline{V}_t(z,u_1) = \int \log\left[\frac{u_2(r-s)+s}{u_1(r-s)+s}\right] p(z;dr) \, .$$

Because $r \to [u_2(r-s)+s]/[u_1(r-s)+s]$ is nondecreasing, the difference function $\overline{V}_t(z,u_2) - \overline{V}_t(z,u_1)$ is nondecreasing (nonincreasing) if p is a monotone (antimonotone) transition probability (cp. Theorem 2.7 and Corollary 2.8). Therefore, for $1 \leq t \leq T$ and for $x \in X$, $z \to f_t(x,z)$ is nondecreasing (nonincreasing).

Because of the monotonic relationship between return r and price z of the risky asset B in the case of the logarithmic utility function, the optimal portfolio policy is also monotone in price z. Although both types of monotonicity of $r(z)$ have their merits, the nonincreasing relationship seems to be of major significance.

We illustrate this by means of a simple example. Suppose at the beginning of each planning period only the prices $z^1 = 80$ and $z^2 = 100$ for asset B are possible. If at the beginning of period t z^1 is realized, the possible returns for period t are $r^{11} = 1$ and $r^{12} = 1.25$; if contrary to this z^2 is obtained, then the possible returns for period t are $r^{21} = 0.8$ and $r^{22} = 1$. That is, a high price z^2 rather leads to a decrease , whereas for the subsequent planning period a high price and thereby also a high return of asset B can be expected from a currently low prize z^1. Independent of the form of both return distributions in this example the disturbance distribution p is in any case antimonotone. Thus, a high price z^2 of the risky asset B implies — because low returns are to be expected — that a smaller proportion is invested in B than in the situation of a low price z^1 at the beginning of the planning period.

This seems to be the appropriate place for a brief discussion of structural properties, like monotonicity, in the theory of dynamic portfolio models. For more general utility functions than those defined in (3,8)– (3,10) it is even for the basic dynamic portfolio model nearly impossible to prove structural properties by means of Lemma 3.7.

In order to guarantee monotonicity of the optimal decision functions $f_t(x)$ with respect to initial wealth x, we must have for the corresponding value functions $\overline{\mathcal{J}}_t(x,u)$ given by (3,12) that $x \to \overline{\mathcal{J}}_t(x,u_2) - \overline{\mathcal{J}}_t(x,u_1)$ is nondecreasing for all $u_1, u_2 \in K$ with $u_1 \leq u_2$. This difference function is nondecreasing in x if the following is true (cp. Bodily/White (1982) and Heyman/Sobel (1984), Theorem 8.5):

$$(3,20) \qquad q(x_2,u_2;E) - q(x_2,u_1;E) \leq q(x_1,u_2;E) - q(x_1,u_1;E)$$

for all increasing sets $E \subseteq X$, $x_1, x_2 \in X$ with $x_1 \leq x_2$ and $u_1, u_2 \in K$ with $u_1 \leq u_2$.

The transition probability q is defined as

$$q(x,u;E) := p(\{r | x[(1-u)s + ur] \in E\}) \ .$$

Consequently by Lemma 3.7 the optimal investment decisions $f_t(x)$, $1 \leq t \leq T$, are nondecreasing functions of the initial wealth x.

It is a difficult, if not impossible task to justify condition (3,20): until now we do not know any family of return distributions which satisfies (3,20).

But defining $E(x,u) := \int x' q(x,u,;dx')$ as the conditional expected initial wealth of planning period $t+1$ given x and u of the running period t, by Theorem 2.7 we have

$$E(x_2,u_2) - E(x_2,u_1) \geq E(x_1,u_2) - E(x_1,u_1),$$

provided that the expected return $E(r)$ of the risky asset B is not less than the return s of the riskless asset A, i.e. $E(r) \geq s$.

The preceding analysis comes to a contrary result compared to the one obtained for utility functions (3,8)–(3,10). Theorem 3.2 together with Theorem 3.6 shows that the optimal investment decision functions $f_t(x)$, $1 \leq t \leq T$, are nonincreasing provided $E(r) \geq s$ holds. But from condition (3,20) we also conclude $E(r) \geq s$; the optimal proportions invested in the risky asset B $f_t(x)$ are in this case nondecreasing functions of the initial wealth x.

What is the conclusion ?
Already Bodily/White (1982) mention in the concluding remarks of their paper the impossibility to verify condition (3,20), if the transition probability q is defined by the transition of wealth $x' = [(1-u)s + ur]x$ and the distribution of the risky return r. From the previously shown contradiction it is evident that for our basic dynamic portfolio model condition (3,20) is never satisfied. Therefore, it is not possible to derive the monotonicity of the optimal investment decisions $f_t(x)$ by means of Lemma 3.7. The only way to prove this structural property for the dynamic portfolio model considered is to employ Theorem 3.6.

Finally to this section on extensions of the basic model we turn to the inclusion of (proportional) transaction costs. For this case Constantinides (1979) shows that the optimal investment policy is of a special form, namely a policy with two control limits t_u and t_0.

Let the initial wealth x of a planning period be composed of $x = x^A + x^B$, where $x^A(x^B)$ is the part of the wealth resulting from the riskless (risky) asset $A(B)$. It is then not optimal to revise the portfolio if $t_u \leq x^B/x^A \leq t_0$ holds.

If instead $x^B/x^A < t_u$ ($> t_0$) the optimal investment policy prescribes how much more (less) to invest in the risky asset B until $t_u(t_0)$ is reached.

This type of control policy consisting of two control limits is interesting at least for two reasons. On the one hand, it is simple and on the other hand, it is often encountered in dynamic stochastic decision models, for example in the field of cash management models (cp. e.g. Elton/Gruber (1979)) and in the field of the so–called production–inventory–models (cp. e.g. Jammernegg (1982)).

3.1.3. Classic Dynamic Portfolio Models under Uncertainty

In the last part of the previous section we have already dealt with the critical assumption of the dynamic portfolio model under risk: As the returns of the risky asset are stochastically independent over time, the investor ignores the information, like asset prices and returns, obtained during the planning process. Therefore, the basic model was extended by the state of the economy z which includes the information of a planning period. Because of the dependence of the return distribution on z the optimal investment decisions are influenced by the state of the economy, too.

The problem involved with this generalized model is, on the one hand, the extension of the state space and, on the other hand, the necessary specification of the disturbance distribution p (see assumption d). In general, the definition of the state of the economy z will be a difficult task; in one example z denotes the price of the risky asset B.

As this example shows, the state of the economy z first of all represents "hard" data. Among them we mean all observable market data, like prices, dividends, returns etc. Not included in the state of the economy are mainly "soft" data like different kinds of verbal information from different individuals, which possibly have an effect on the risk attitudes of the investor expressed by the distribution of returns.

These "soft" data might be of special meaning for small investors as the information obtained e.g. by consulting an expert is in verbal form rather than in the form of probability statements. These pieces of advice may contain information reaching from the individual firm and industry level to governmental decisions and international developments (cp. for this subject Winkler (1979)).

We now assume that the naive investor considered knows the family of distributions of the return of the risky asset B, but does not know all parameters of this distribution. In the following one parameter is taken as unknown at the beginning of the investment process. The investor is in the position to condense the "soft" subjective information perhaps together with "hard" past data, i.e. already observed returns, to a prior distribution for this unknown parameter.

At the beginning of each planning period the actual "hard" data, i.e. the return of the previous period, are used to update the return distribution of the risky asset B by means of Bayes' theorem. If the revision of the probability distribution is desirable as new information arrives, the Bayesian approach seems to be a well–suited instrument for the analysis of such sequential decision models (cp. Winkler (1973), Dhingra (1983)).

Dynamic Bayesian portfolio models were for the first time considered by Winkler/Barry (1975) and Winkler (1979). These papers only contain a fundamental discussion of the assumptions to the model and write down the value iteration equations of dynamic programming. A detailed analysis is presented by Kischka (1984), chapter 3.

As the name of the model already indicates, the proper framework for the analysis is Bayesian dynamic programming (cp. Rieder (1975a)). Essentially the original Bayesian model is reduced to an ordinary stochastic dynamic program of the type used in this work. In this case the state of the economy z represents the posterior return distribution $p(n, y; \cdot)$ of the risky asset as defined in (2,5).

But we restrict the attention to the distributions from Table 2.1, the Bernoulli, Gamma, Lognormal and Normal distribution. It is therefore not necessary to define the state of the economy as the whole posterior distribution. As for these distributions one–dimensional sufficient statistics exist, it is enough to use the information state (n, y) defined in chapter 2 as state of the economy z.

Thus, we describe the original dynamic Bayesian portfolio model in its reduced form by means of the already known stochastic dynamic program.

In analogy to the random variables X_i, $1 \leq i \leq n$, of chapter 2, we assume now in generalizing assumption A3 that the stochastic returns $r_{-L}, \ldots, r_T$ of asset B constitute for given parameter $\theta \in \Theta$ a sequence of *iid* random variables with probability distribution ν_θ. At the beginning of the decision process, i.e. at the beginning of period one, there may exist "hard" data as prior information. They are represented by the sample of returns $(r_{-L}, \ldots, r_0)$, $L \in \mathbf{N}_0$. At the beginning of planning period

t, $1 \le t \le T$, the information state (n, y) is then given by the sufficient statistic $y = T(r_{-L}, \ldots, r_{t-1})$ and $n = L + t$.

If no returns of the risky asset B are used as prior information, the information state (n, y) is specified at the beginning of period one as $(0, y_0)$ and in the subsequent planning periods $t = 2, \ldots, T$ by the sufficient statistic $y = T(r_1, \ldots, r_{t-1})$ and $n = t - 1$. For the distributions of Table 2.1 we have either $y_0 = 0$ (additive sufficient statistic) or $y_0 = 1$ (multiplicative sufficient statistic).

If we define the prior distribution for the unknown parameter θ by $\overline{\mu}$ and if the information state (n, y) has been obtained, the posterior distribution is given by the transition probability (tp) $\mu(n, y; \cdot)$ from (2,4), whereas the posterior distribution for return r_t is characterized by the tp $p(n, y; \cdot)$ from (2,5).

Therefore, we can describe the dynamic Bayesian portfolio model like in section 3.1.2.3 as the tupel $(X \times Z, K, D, p, w, \overline{v}, U)$ where the following elements are specified in a concrete form:

a) $Z = \mathbf{N}_0 \times \mathbf{R}$; $(n, y) \in Z$ denotes the information state (state of the economy) at the beginning of a planning period,
b) the disturbance distribution p is a transition probability from Z to D defined in (2,5),
c) $\overline{v} : Z \times D \to Z$ determines the transformation of the information state between two subsequent planning periods. It is given by $\overline{v}(n, y, r) = (n+1, v(y, r))$, where the recursion function v is defined in (2,7).

If at the beginning of planning period t the information state is (n, y), then the information state of the subsequent period $t + 1$ is characterized by $n + 1$ observations and the sufficient statistic $T(r_{-L}, \ldots, r_t) = v(T(r_{-L}, \ldots, r_{t-1}), r_t)$, provided $y = T(r_{-L}, \ldots, r_{t-1})$.

If analogous conditions as those of subsection 3.1.2.3 hold, the value functions of dynamic programming (3,17) and (3,18) are of the following specific form:

$$\mathcal{J}_{T+1}(x, n, y) = U(x)$$

and for $1 \le t \le T$

$$\overline{\mathcal{J}}_t(x, n, y, u) = \int \mathcal{J}_{t+1}\left(\left[(1 - u)s + ur\right] x, n + 1, v(y, r)\right) p(n, y; dr)$$

(3,21)

$$\mathcal{J}_t(x, n, y) = \max_{u \in K} \overline{\mathcal{J}}_t(x, n, y, u)\,.$$

The optimal investment decisions $f_t(x,n,y)$, defined by

$$(3,22) \qquad \mathcal{J}_t(x,n,y) = \overline{\mathcal{J}}_t(x,n,y,f_t(x,n,y))$$

in this situation clearly depend on the information state (n, y).
An essential advantage of the dynamic portfolio model under conditions of uncertainty, given by (3,21) and (3,22), against the extended dynamic portfolio model under conditions of risk, defined by (3,17) and (3,18), is the "natural" way of obtaining the transition probabilities $p(n,y;\cdot)$. The adjective "natural" is a paraphrase for the theorem of Bayes. The price that has to be paid is the specification of a prior distribution for the unknown parameter θ of the return distribution $\nu_\theta, \theta \in \Theta$. By restriction to natural conjugate prior distributions, the a priori "known" parameters of the distribution can be computed e.g. by means of the procedure described at the end of chapter 2.

It is of course a challenging task to compare the optimal investment decisions of the Bayesian investor with those of the investor who behaves according to the basic dynamic portfolio model of subsection 3.1.2.2. Jennings/Barry (1983) as well as Kischka (1984) use for this purpose the so-called hybrid model that is characterized by an exponential utility function of final wealth (3,8) $U(x) = -\exp(-x/a)$. In the hybrid model the return distribution of the risky asset B is the normal distribution, i.e. $r \sim N(\theta, \sigma^2)$, where θ is the unknown expectation parameter and σ^2 is the known variance. The assumption of a known variance σ^2 of the distribution of return r is confirmed by the theoretical and empirical studies of Oldfield/Rogalski/Jarrow (1977) and Kallberg/Ziemba (1984).

The previously mentioned comparison of the optimal proportions invested in the risky asset B is even for these special assumptions connected with considerable numerical difficulties. Kischka therefore chooses in his example a non-informative (diffuse) prior distribution for the unknown parameter θ (for non-informative prior distributions cp. e.g. Berger (1985), section 3.3). For the two-period model ($T = 2$) it is shown that in the first planning period the Bayesian investor puts less into the risky asset B than an investor with independent, identically Normal-distributed returns (cp. Kischka (1984), pp. 122).

In the following we consider a special informative prior distribution, namely the conjugate Normal distribution, i.e. $\theta \sim N(\mu, \tau^2)$. It is assumed that the "prior sample" $(r_{-L}, \dots, r_0)$ of hard data is already incorporated in the prior distribution. The computation of the optimal Bayesian investment decisions is in this case even for the two–period model extremely difficult. We therefore choose another line of comparison.

Investor I ignores the returns obtained during the planning process, i.e. he starts from *iid* returns of the risky asset B. Due to the previous remarks, at the beginning of planning period one the information state (n, y) is given by $(0,0)$. Thus, it seems reasonable that the investor uses the corresponding posterior distribution for all planning periods, i.e. $r_t \sim N(\mu, \sigma^2 + \tau^2)$, $t = 1, \ldots, T$ (see Table 2.2).

Subsequently to Corollary 3.3 we already considered the dynamic portfolio model with utility function which expresses constant absolute risk aversion and with normally distributed returns, though with known parameters. If the nonstationary returns are normally distributed $r_t \sim N(\mu_t, \sigma_t^2)$, the optimal proportions invested in asset B are $f_t(x) = a/(xs^{T-t})(\mu_t - s)/\sigma_t^2$, $t = 1, \ldots, T$.

With that we arrive at the following portfolio decisions for investor I:

$$(3,23) \qquad f_t^I(x) = a/\left(xs^{T-t}\right)(\mu - s)/(\sigma^2 + \tau^2), \quad t = 1, \ldots, T\ .$$

Investor II differs from the Bayesian investor by only taking into account the possibility of reinvesting the wealth but by not considering the fact that by means of future returns the corresponding distributions can be revised. Such a suboptimal behaviour, or correctly non–optimal behaviour, where the decision is computed using past information but as if no further information will be received in the future, is known in control theory as "open–loop feedback control policy" (cp. Bertsekas (1976), pp. 198).

Thus, the only difference between investor II and investor I lies in the return distribution of the risky asset B. For investor II in planning period t this distribution is given by the posterior distribution $p(n, y;\, dr)$ with $n := t - 1$, i.e. $r_t \sim N(\mu(n, y), \sigma^2 + \tau_n^2)$ and the parameters $\mu(n, y)$ and τ_n^2 are specified in Table 2.2.

For $1 \leq t \leq T$ the optimal portfolio decision for investor II is:

$$(3,24) \quad f_t^{II}(x, n, y) = a/\left(xs^{T-t}\right)\left[\tau^2(y - ns) + \sigma^2(\mu - s)\right]/\left[\sigma^4 + (n+1)\sigma^2\tau^2\right].$$

We immediately see from (3,23) that investor I puts his money into the risky asset B if the expected return of B is higher than the return of the riskless asset A, i.e. if $E(r) = \mu > s$ holds.

Investor II, however, also takes into consideration the past returns obtained during the planning process. Therefore, we can identify in (3,24) one expression concerning the present, $\sigma^2(\mu - s)$, and another expression concerning the past, $\tau^2(y - ns)$, such that $\mu > s$ is not sufficient for investment in asset B.

We are of course interested in the question when the adaptive investor II puts more money into the risky asset than his opponent investor I. When does $f_t^{II}(x,n,y) > f_t^I(x)$ hold ?
The answer is, if and only if

$$y > n(\tau^2 s + \sigma^2 \mu)/(\sigma^2 + \tau^2)$$

is satisfied.

A look to Table 2.2 shows that in case of the Normal distribution $\mu(1,s) = (\tau^2 s + \sigma^2 \mu)/(\sigma^2 + \tau^2)$.

So in planning period t investor II puts more into the risky asset B than investor I, if the arithmetic mean of past returns $y/n = (r_1 + \cdots + r_{t-1})/n$ is higher than the conditional expected return of a planning period, provided the observed return of asset B is always equal to the return s of the riskless asset A.

The interpretation becomes more clear in the case the prior expected return of asset B is equal to the return of asset A, i.e. if $\mu = s$ holds. The optimal portfolio policy for investor I in this situation is always to put all the initial wealth of a period into the riskless asset A. But investor II decides to invest in the risky asset B, if the arithmetic mean of past returns y/n is higher than the riskless return s. Thus, risky investment pays if the past returns of asset B are on average higher than the return of the riskless asset A.

As a final part of this section we make some comments on the existence of structural properties of the optimal Bayesian investment policy, defined in (3,22). Contrary to the extended dynamic portfolio model with general state of the economy z (see subsection 3.1.2.3), in the Bayesian dynamic portfolio model wealth x and information state (n, y) are closely related. Therefore, it is of no use investigating the monotonicity of $f_t(x,n,y)$ with respect to x separated from that with respect to (n, y).

The only exception again is the model with logarithmic utility of final wealth $\log x$. As the analysis subsequent to Lemma 3.7 shows, in this case the optimal proportion $f_t(x,n,y)$ invested in the risky asset B is independent of wealth x. Thus, it makes sense to check whether $f_t(x,n,y)$ is monotone in the information state (n,y).

In order to employ Lemma 3.7 we have for $z=(n,y)$:

$$\overline{V}_t(n,y,u_2)-\overline{V}_t(n,y,u_1)=\int \log\left[\frac{u_2(r-s)+s}{u_1(r-s)+s}\right]\ p(n,y;\,dr)\ .$$

We already mentioned in the analysis subsequent to Lemma 3.7 that the function in brackets is nondecreasing in r. Now $p(n,y;\cdot)$ is a monotone transition probability by Theorem 2.13. Then by means of Lemma 3.7 and Theorem 2.7 it follows that the Bayesian investment decisions $f_t(x,n,y)$ are nondecreasing in the information state (n,y). That is, better information with respect to the asset B causes the investor to put a higher proportion of the initial wealth of a planning period into the risky asset B: The higher the past returns of asset B, the more risky is the present investment decision.

This is the only structural result we are able to obtain for the Bayesian investor. This "lack of structure" of the optimal portfolio policy is one reason that in the following we are dealing with the binary Bayesian portfolio model, which has already been briefly sketched in the introduction of this chapter. There the only decision the investor has, is whether to put all the initial wealth of a planning period into the riskless asset A or into the risky asset B.

3.2 Binary Dynamic Portfolio Models under Uncertainty

In this section we are dealing with the binary Bayesian dynamic portfolio model that we have already sketched in the introduction to this chapter; a model mainly meant for small investors who have to decide whether to invest part of their savings in a risky asset, say a stock. Having in mind the goal of maximizing the expected (utility of) final wealth, the investor in each of a finite number of planning periods has to make the decision whether to reinvest or to sell the risky asset. He does so on the basis of his adaptive behaviour by continuously taking into account the actual return of the risky asset. Apart from these objective data also subjective risk preferences and beliefs of the investor are considered in the decision process. This is achieved by means of a prior distribution of a parameter of the return distribution of the risky asset that a priori is assumed to be unknown. These "hard" and "soft" information is used to compute the actual posterior return distribution via Bayes' theorem.

It seems to be necessary to discuss two things of the introductory remarks in more detail. One thing is the "bracketed" utility function and the other one is the consideration of the subjective risk attitudes by the prior distribution. One main feature of the binary portfolio model is that we are not interested in diversification of the two assets in the usual sense which in the previous section 3.1 in general has been achieved by specifying a strictly concave, nondecreasing utility function. Thus, we may start from a linear utility function of final wealth and instead include risk aversion of the investor in the model by the choice of the type of the risky asset's return distribution and first of all by the specification of the prior distribution. This is done not only by the variance but also by the skewness and the kurtosis of the distribution. We will come back to this point in more detail by discussing the choice of the families of return distributions in the next subsection.

But we are also dealing with the binary portfolio model with utility functions expressing constant relative risk aversion, e.g. the logarithmic utility function. For the case of the two–point–return distribution we demonstrate the different effects on the optimal investment decisions, on the one hand, by risk averse utility functions and, on the other hand, by risk averse, i.e. positively skewed return distributions. We anticipate one result: The "square–root" investor does not differ at all with respect to the optimal portfolio policy from the "linear investor". And there is almost no difference between "logarithmic" and "linear" investors.

At the end of section 3.1.3 by discussing the classic Bayesian dynamic portfolio model we had to notice disappointedly that it is almost impossible to prove structural properties of the optimal investment–decisions. In the comparatively more simple binary model — diversification is not allowed within a planning period, but only over time — we are able to obtain under quite plausible assumptions such structural properties which in our opinion can be often observed in practice. These results are not extremely surprising for us because the binary Bayesian dynamic portfolio model is in some sense an extension of the well–known one–armed bandit models (cp. for the latter e.g. Hengartner/Kalin/Theodorescu (1981), Kolonko/Benzing (1985), Benzing/ Theodorescu (1985), Berry/Fristedt (1985)).

After specifying the model in detail and formulating it as a stochastic dynamic program in section 3.2.2, we are dealing in the subsequent section with structural properties of the optimal investment policy: There holds a stopping rule for the risky asset whose distribution depends a priori on an unkown parameter. If in a planning period the investor decides to sell the risky asset, he does not revise this decision until the planning horizon. This behaviour seems to be plausible for a small investor: If he has made rather bad experience with investing in a risky asset, then this disappointment besides others will be manifested by the fact that he will keep his money on the savings account for a while, in this case at least until the planning horizon.

Furthermore, the optimal investment decisions are nondecreasing in the information state. Better information, expressed by high past returns, causes the investor to behave more risky.

Moreover, for the interesting special case of a two–point return distribution of the risky asset holds the stay–on–a–winner–property, whose name stems from the bandit models: If in a planning period the investor earns the "high" return of the risky asset, then in the subsequent planning period he will invest risky again.

3.2.1 The Return Distribution of the Risky Asset

In the binary portfolio model we are dealing with rather unusual distributions for the returns of the risky asset B. Therefore, we will have a look upon this choice from a theoretical as well as empirical point of view. We restrict the discussion of the return distribution of the risky asset B to securities, say a stock.

Remember the definition of the return r_t of B in planning period t, given in (3,1), namely $r_t = (P_{t+1} + D_t)/P_t$, where P_τ denotes the stock price at the beginning of planning period τ and D_t are dividend payments in period t. Then the rate of return is just defined by $r_t - 1$ (cp. e.g. Philippatos (1979), p. 313).

By the way, there is no agreement which variable should describe the security. Besides the return and the rate of return, the price of the security itself as well as the difference of subsequent prices and the difference of the logarithmic prices are taken into consideration. One essential point is for which of these variables an easy to work with probability distribution can be specified; this leads to the subject of empirical investigations (cp. Winkler (1973)). From an economic point of view it seems to be reasonable to use the return or the rate of return as variable for the model instead of simply taking the price differences (cp. Fama (1976), p. 19).

The rate of return mainly is chosen for empirical investigations. Pioneering research has been done by Fama (cp. Fama (1976), chapter 1). He starts by assuming that the rates of return constitute an *iid* sequence of normally distributed random variables. The empirical investigations are done both for daily and monthly data. The empirical density of the daily data shows a leptokurtic behaviour, i.e. a positive kurtosis: The frequency distribution has more mass around its arithmetic mean and fat tails compared to the Normal distribution. These empirically observed fat tails of the distribution of the daily rates of return lead to the conjecture that the return distribution has no finite second moment, i.e. that it has an infinite variance. Therefore, the family of stable symmetric distributions was considered as another candidate for the distribution of the rate of return. This family is characterized by the fact that the sum of *iid* stable random variables is again a stable random variable. The two most prominent representators are the Normal distribution and the Cauchy distribution. An exact definition and properties of stable distributions can be found e.g. in Patel/Kapadia/Owen (1976), pp. 100.

The empirical estimation of the parameters of the stable distribution not surprisingly resulted in such estimates that for the return distribution no variance exists.

Perry gave another explanation for the observed fat tails: The variance is finite but non–stationary over time (cp. Perry (1983), where a good summary of the current discussion concerning the specification of the return distribution can be found).

The empirical investigations of the daily rates of return always tacitly assume a symmertric distribution. In course of checking the monthly data Fama also takes a possible asymmetry, i.e. skewness, of the distribution of the rate of return into consideration (Fama (1976), pp. 26). Actually a slight positive skewness of the frequency distribution has been encountered. Furthermore, a slight leptokurtic behaviour of the distribution has been observed which, however, is weaker than that of the daily data. Despite these empirical findings the Normal distribution is used as an approximative working hypothesis.

Now it is no point of discussion that the shape of the return distribution of the security decisively expresses the investor's risk preferences. Furthermore, there is no controversy that positively skewed return distributions are more "risky" than symmetric and negatively skewed distributions with the same expected value and the same variance. In other words: Distributions with positive skewness reflect risk averse attitudes of the investor (cp. e.g. Swoboda (1981), p. 104).

An important aspect of asymmetric return distributions is confirmed theoretically as well as empirically by Simkowitz and Beedles (1978). Suppose the return distributions are positively skewed. Then the larger the number of securities of a portfolio is, the less is the (positive) skewness of the distribution of the portfolio. Simkowitz and Beedles used the monthly returns over twenty years of 549 stocks which are continuously traded at the New York Stock Exchange for their investigations. The distributions of the returns of these 549 stocks showed on average a positive skewness. They randomly selected 5–stock–portfolios. In this way on average 80 % of the unsystematic risk, expressed by the variance of the portfolio, is diversified away. But also on average more than 92 % of the skewness are eliminated by the considered 5–stock–portfolios (cp. Simkowitz/Beedles (1978), pp. 935).

The consequence: The majority of privat investors has no perfectly diversified portfolios – an often observed phenomenon (cp. e.g. Kane (1982), pp. 15). One possible explanation for this observed behaviour might be that investors want to document their risk preferences by means of positively skewed return distributions; and this skewness–property is destroyed by diversification.

The preceding remarks are in our opinion a plausible justification to allow only for diversification over time and not for diversification in the usual sense, because risk attitudes are first of all included in the binary portfolio model via return distributions with positive skewness.

The lack of statistical models for testing asymmetric distributions is one reason that besides these empirical findings mainly the Normal distribution is used as distribution of the return of a security (There are exceptions in nonparametric statistics, cp. e.g. for positively skewed distributions Hogg/Fisher/Randles (1975)).

We summarize with a statement that is in our opinion characteristic for the choice of a return distribution. In their textbook Brealey and Myers specify the Normal distribution as the distribution of the return of a stock. Afterwards they comment in a footnote: "There is, however, one way in which we have cheated. If you were to measure returns over a long interval, the distribution will be skewed. You would encounter rates of returns greater than 100 percent but none less than –100 percent" (Brealey/Myers (1981), p. 134, footnote 2).

Thus, we concentrate on return distributions with nonnegative support as well as positive skewness and also positive kurtosis. Because we are starting from a return distribution that initially depends on an unknown parameter which is updated in a Bayesian manner, we restrict ourselves for the matter of presentation to the Gamma distribution and to the Lognormal distribution. Furthermore, we discuss the binary portfolio model with a two-point distribution of the return of the risky security B, because in this case we can develop a simple algorithm for computing the optimal investment policy.

3.2.2 The Stochastic Dynamic Program

After the verbal presentation of the binary Bayesian dynamic portfolio model as well as a detailed discussion concerning the choice of the probability distribution of the return of the risky asset B, similarly to the classic model (see section 3.1.2.1) we now put together the basic assumptions for the binary model. Afterwards we describe the model as a stochastic dynamic program and show some important properties.

3.2.2.1 Assumptions

B1. There are no transaction costs and taxes. The riskless asset A and the risky asset B are completely divisible.

B2. The investor maximizes the expected utility of final wealth x_{T+1} over T planning periods. The increasing, concave utility function U has constant relative risk aversion.

Because of a more simple presentation we choose contrary to (3,9) and (3,10) the following form of the utility functions:

(3,25) logarithmic : $U(x) = \log x$

(3,26) power : $U(x) = x^c/c\ , \quad c \leq 1$

The measure of relative risk aversion is given by $R(x) = 1 - c$. The comparison with (3,9) and (3,10) shows that $1/b = 1 - c$. The important special case of the linear utility function is characterized by $c = 1$, i.e. $R(x) = 0$. The logarithmic utility function (3,25) is in the sense of relative risk aversion the limiting case of the power utility functions as c goes to zero. We will need this relationship in course of the empirical sensitivity analysis.

B3. The return s of the riskless asset remains constant over all T planning periods, and it holds:

$$s \geq 1 \ . \tag{3,27}$$

B4. $r_t, -L \leq t \leq T$, is the non-negative random return of the risky asset B in planning period t. The returns $r_{-L}, \ldots, r_0, L \in \mathbf{N}_0$, are the prior information of "hard" data at the beginning of the planning process.
The probability distribution ν_θ of the random return r_t depends on an unknown parameter $\theta \in \Theta \subseteq \mathbf{R}$. In the following we asume ν_θ to be either the Gamma, the Lognormal or the two-point distribution with values $r1$, $r2$, $r1 > r2 \geq 0$ (see Table 2.1).
Given the parameter $\theta \in \Theta$, the returns $r_{-L}, \ldots, r_T$ constitute an *iid* sequence of random variables with distribution ν_θ (cp. for this assumption Fama (1976), chapter 4).

From chapter 2 we already know that at the beginning of planning period t, $1 \leq t \leq T$, in any case a one-dimensional sufficient statistic $y = T(r_{-L}, \ldots, r_{t-1})$ exists. The information state again can be represented by the pair (n, y), where $n := L + t$.

In the case ν_θ is the two-point distribution (n, y) indicates the number of high returns $r1$ observed in a sample of size n.

If at the beginning of the planning process there is no prior information of returns of the risky asset B available, then the information state is specified in the case of the Gamma and the two-point distribution by $(0, 0)$, and in the case of the Lognormal distribution by $(0, 1)$ due to the multiplicative sufficient statistic.

B5. The investor behaves in a Bayesian manner. He is also in the position to condense the "soft" data to the prior distribution $\overline{\mu}$ for the unknown parameter θ. Given information state (n, y), at the beginning of planning period t, the posterior distribution μ for θ is characterized by the transition probability (*tp*) $\mu(n, y; .)$ defined by (2,4). The corresponding posterior distribution of return r_t of the risky asset B is specified by the *tp* $p(n, y; .)$ from (2,5).

We define the expected power and logarithmic return, respectively, of asset B for one monetary unit, given information state (n, y), by:

$$E_c(n, y) := \int r^c / c \, p(n, y; dr) \ , \tag{3,28}$$

$$E_\ell(n,y) := \int \log r \, p(n,y;\, dr)\,. \tag{3,29}$$

B6. The investor is only diversifying over time. At the beginning of each planning period he has to decide to put all the wealth either into asset A or into asset B. The whole wealth obtained in this way is reinvested in the subsequent planning period.

B7. The investor revises the information state concerning the risky asset B over the T planning periods if and only if he is investing in a planning period in B.

This assumption is decisive for proving the structural properties of the optimal portfolio policy ("stop–loss-policy"). We will discuss it later on in detail.

Finally we comment assumption B3: We specified asset A as a riskless asset. But the results of this chapter remain true if the return s of asset A is a nonnegative random variable with known distribution, provided it is independent of the random parameter θ as well as of the random returns $r_{-L}, \ldots, r_T$ of asset B (cp. for this Jammernegg (1985)). Especially the latter point — the independence of the random returns of different assets — often is (partly reasonable) questioned. This axiom of independence might at least be satisfied for securities from different industries. With that it is guaranteed that e.g. in the one–period model the optimal portfolio possesses some fundamental structural properties (cp. first of all McEntire (1984)).

3.2.2.2 Fundamental Properties

We now formulate the binary dynamic Bayesian portfolio model as a stochastic dynamic program under conditions of risk. Subsequently we show that like in the classic portfolio model the optimal investment decisions are independent of the initial wealth of a planning period because of assumption B2. Furthermore, by assumption B4 the value functions of dynamic programming are nondecreasing with respect to the information state (n, y).

The assumptions B1 to B7 lead to the following stochastic dynamic program represented by the tupel $(X \times Z, K, D, w, p, U)$:

a) the state space $X \times Z := \mathbf{R}^+ \times \mathbf{N}_0 \times \mathbf{R}^+$; $x \in X$ is the initial wealth of a planning period and $(n, y) \in Z$ denotes the information state at the beginning of a planning period. In the case of a two–

point distribution of the return of the risky asset B clearly we have $Z = \mathbf{N}_0^2$.

b) the action space $K := \{1, 2\}$; action 1(2) means in the running planning period investment in asset $A(B)$.

c) the disturbance space $D := \mathbf{R}^+$; $r \in D$ denotes the (random) return of asset $A(B)$ of a planning period.

d) the state transition $w : X \times Z \times K \times D \to X \times Z$, where

$$w(x, n, y; 1; s) = (sx; n, y) \quad \text{and}$$
$$w(x, n, y; 2; r) = (rx; n + 1, v(y, r))$$

in the case of the Gamma and the Lognormal distribution. The recursion function v is defined by (2,7).

For the two–point distribution of the return of the risky asset B we define:

$$v(y, r1) := y + 1 \quad \text{and}$$
(3,30) $$v(y, r2) := y\,.$$

e) the disturbance distribution p is a transition probability from Z to D, which is defined in (2,5) and which denotes the posterior return distribution of asset B.
In the case of the two–point distribution we meet the same notational convention for the posterior probability of obtaining the high return $r1$ of asset B as for the Bernoulli distribution (2,10):

(3,31) $$p(n, y) := p(n, y; \{r1\})\,.$$

f) the final reward function $U : X \to \mathbf{R}$ represents the utility of wealth at the end of planning period T, the planning horizon; it is given by (3,25) and (3,26), respectively.

For positive initial wealth at the beginning of the planning process the value functions $V_t : X \times Z \to \mathbf{R}$ are well defined. They denote the maximal expected reward from planning period t onwards, $1 \leq t \leq T+1$. Then the optimality equations of dynamic programming are given in the following way:

$$V_t(x,n,y) = \mathrm{Max}\{V_t^1(x,n,y),\ V_t^2(x,n,y)\}\ ,\quad 1 \le t \le T\,,$$
$$V_{T+1}(x,n,y) = U(x)$$

where

$$V_t^1(x,n,y) = V_{t+1}(sx,n,y)$$

and

$$V_t^2(x,n,y) = \int V_{t+1}(rx, n+1, v(y,r))\ p(n,y;\ dr).$$

We already know from the classic dynamic portfolio models of section 3.1 that the optimal investment decisions are independent of the initial wealth if the utility function U has constant relative risk aversion. As we consider here only the utility functions (3,25) and (3,26) which obey this property, we define in the following value functions with constant initial wealth of a planning period $x = 1$.

The value functions $\mathcal{J}_t : Z \to \mathbf{R}$ denote for constant initial wealth $x = 1$ the maximal expected reward from planning period t onwards, $1 \le t \le T+1$. The optimality equations of dynamic programming are as follows:

(3,32)
$$\mathcal{J}_t(n,y) = \mathrm{Max}\{\mathcal{J}_t^1(n,y),\ \mathcal{J}_t^2(n,y)\},\quad 1 \le t \le T\,,$$
$$\mathcal{J}_{T+1}(n,y) = U(1)\,,$$

where for the logarithmic utility function (3,25) $U(x) = \log x$:

(3,33)
$$\mathcal{J}_t^1(n,y) = \log s + \mathcal{J}_{t+1}(n,y)\ ,$$
$$\mathcal{J}_t^2(n,y) = E_\ell(n,y) + \int \mathcal{J}_{t+1}(n+1, v(y,r))p(n,y;\ dr).$$

For the power utility functions (3,26) $U(x) = x^c/c\,, 0 < c \le 1$, we have:

$$\mathcal{J}_t^1(n,y) = s^c\,\mathcal{J}_{t+1}(n,y)$$

(3,34)
$$\mathcal{J}_t^2(n,y) = \int r^c\,\mathcal{J}_{t+1}(n+1, v(y,r))p(n,y;\ dr)\ .$$

The next lemma shows the relationship of the value functions V_t and $\mathcal{J}_t$:

LEMMA 3.8. *For $1 \le t \le T$ and $(x,n,y) \in X \times Z$ we have*

a) *for the logarithmic utility function $U(x) = \log x$:*
   i) $V_t^a(x,n,y) = \log x + \mathcal{J}_t^a(n,y)$, $\quad a = 1,2$,
   ii) $V_t(x,n,y) = \log x + \mathcal{J}_t(n,y)$.

b) *for the power utility functions $U(x) = x^c/c, 0 < c \le 1$:*
   i) $V_t^a(x,n,y) = x^c \mathcal{J}_t^a(n,y)$, $\quad a = 1,2$,
   ii) $V_t(x,n,y) = x^c \mathcal{J}_t(n,y)$.

PROOF. *We use simultaneous backward induction over i) and ii). Only part a) is shown.*

1) *Let $t = T$. Then we have:*

$$V_T^1(x,n,y) = \log x + \log s = \log x + \mathcal{J}_T^1(n,y),$$
$$V_T^2(x,n,y) = \int \log(rx)p(n,y;\,dr) = \log x + E_\ell(n,y)$$
$$= \log x + \mathcal{J}_T^2(n,y)$$

and thus $V_T(x,n,y) = \log x + \mathcal{J}_T(n,y)$.

2) *Let i) and ii) be true for $t+1 \le \tau \le T$; then we have:*

$$V_t^1(x,n,y) = \log(sx) + \mathcal{J}_{t+1}(n,y) = \log x + \mathcal{J}_t^1(n,y),$$
$$V_t^2(x,n,y) = \int [\log(rx) + \mathcal{J}_{t+1}(n+1, v(y,r))]p(n,y;\,dr)$$
$$= \log x + E_\ell(n,y) + \int \mathcal{J}_{t+1}(n+1, v(y,r))p(n,y;\,dr)$$
$$= \log x + \mathcal{J}_t^2(n,y),$$

and thus $\quad V_t(x,n,y) = \log x + \mathcal{J}_t(n,y)$.

Lemma 3.8 guarantees that also in the binary dynamic portfolio model the optimal investment decisions are independent of the initial wealth of a planning period. Thus, we may restrict ourselves in the following to the value functions $\mathcal{J}_t$ with constant initial wealth $x = 1$, thereby reducing the dimension of the state space by one.

Therefore, for $1 \le t \le T$ and $(n,y) \in Z$ the optimal binary portfolio policy is a finite sequence of investment decision functions $f_t : Z \to K$ defined as follows:

$$f_t(n,y) = \begin{cases} 1 & \mathcal{J}_t^1(n,y) > \mathcal{J}_t^2(n,y) \\ 2 & \mathcal{J}_t^1(n,y) \le \mathcal{J}_t^2(n,y)\,. \end{cases} \tag{3,35}$$

If $\mathcal{J}_t^1(n,y) = \mathcal{J}_t^2(n,y)$ then $f_t(n,y) = 2$, i.e. the wealth is put into the risky asset B.

For proving the structural properties of the optimal binary portfolio policy (3,35) it is necessary to show the monotonicity of the value functions, defined by (3,32) – (3,34), with respect to the information state (n,y) (cp. (2,8) and (2,8')).

LEMMA 3.9. *For $1 \le t \le T$ and $(n,y) \le (n',y')$ in the sense of (2,8) and (2,8'), respectively, we have:*

a) $\mathcal{J}_t^a(n,y) \le \mathcal{J}_t^a(n',y')\,, \quad a = 1,2,$
b) $\mathcal{J}_t(n,y) \le \mathcal{J}_t(n',y')$.

PROOF. *We prove the assertion only for the power value functions (3,32) and (3,34) by simultaneous backward induction over a) and b). The proof for the logarithmic value functions (3,32) and (3,33) goes along the same lines.*

1) *Let $t = T$. Then clearly $\mathcal{J}_T^1(n,y) = s^c/c = \mathcal{J}_T^1(n',y')$. Because p is a monotone transition probability (tp) (see chapter 2), we have by Theorem 2.7:*

$$\mathcal{J}_T^2(n,y) = E_c(n,y) \le E_c(n',y') = \mathcal{J}_T^2(n',y')\,.$$

From (3,32) we immediately conclude $\mathcal{J}_T(n,y) \le \mathcal{J}_T(n',y')$.

2) *Let a) and b) be true for $t+1 \le \tau \le T$. Then we have $\mathcal{J}_t^1(n,y) \le \mathcal{J}_t^1(n',y')$, and*

$$\begin{aligned}\mathcal{J}_t^2(n,y) &= \int r^c \mathcal{J}_{t+1}(n+1, v(y,r))p(n,y;\,dr)\\ &\le \int r^c \mathcal{J}_{t+1}(n'+1, v(y',r))p(n,y;\,dr)\\ &\le \int r^c \mathcal{J}_{t+1}(n'+1, v(y',r))p(n',y';\,dr)\\ &= \mathcal{J}_t^2(n',y')\,.\end{aligned}$$

The first inequality is true because the recursion function $v(y,r)$ defined in (2,7) and in (3,30), respectively, is nondecreasing in its first coordinate.

The second inequality holds by using Theorem 2.7 because v is also nondecreasing with respect to its second coordinate and because p is a monotone tp. Therefore we also have $\mathcal{J}_t(n,y) \leq \mathcal{J}_t(n',y')$.

In the proof of the preceding lemma we had to employ assumption B4, which states that the return r of the risky asset B is a nonnegative random variable.

Another auxiliary result is a lower bound for the value functions $\mathcal{J}_t^1$. We do not go through the simple proof by backward induction.

LEMMA 3.10. *For $1 \leq t \leq T$ and $(n,y) \in Z$ we have*

a) *for the logarithmic utility function $U(x) = \log x$:*

$$\mathcal{J}_t^1(n,y) \geq (T+1-t)\log s \ ,$$

b) *for the power utility functions $U(x) = x^c/c, 0 < c \leq 1$:*

$$\mathcal{J}_t^1(n,y) \geq s^{c(T+1-t)}/c \ .$$

Finally we present a property of the posterior probability $p(n,y)$ defined by (3,31) for the model with the two–point return distribution of asset B.

LEMMA 3.11. *For $(n,y) \in Z$ we have:*

$$p(n,y) = p(n,y)p(n+1,y+1) + [1-p(n,y)]p(n+1,y) \, .$$

PROOF. *Let $g(a,b) := \int_0^1 t^a(1-t)^b \, \overline{\mu}(dt)$.*
Then $p(n,y) = g(y+1,n-y)/g(y,n-y)$. Now the assertion immediately follows by collecting terms.

3.2.3 Properties of the Optimal Investment Policy

In this subsection — the central part of the binary dynamic portfolio model — we are going to prove the structural properties of the optimal investment policy, defined in (3,35). These are the stopping rule, the monotonicity of the optimal investment decision functions with respect to the information state and the stay–on–a–winner–property, if the return distribution of asset B is a two–point distribution. For that purpose we extend a technique — the monotonicity of the difference of the value functions of dynamic programming with respect to time — which has been developed for proving similar properties of one–armed bandit models (cp. Kolonko/Benzing (1985) and Benzing/Kolonko (1987)).

We use for the following the difference of the value functions

$$(3,36) \qquad d_t(n,y) := \mathcal{J}_t^2(n,y) - \mathcal{J}_t^1(n,y)\,, \quad 1 \le t \le T, (n,y) \in Z\,.$$

From (3,35) we immediately see that $d_t(n,y) < 0$ is equivalent to $f_t(n,y) = 1$.

Besides from B1 to B7 we additionally need the following assumptions in order to prove the previously mentioned monotonicity over time; subsequently they are assumed to hold.

For the logarithmic utility function $U(x) = \log x$ we have for $(n,y) \in Z$:

$$(L) \qquad \int E_\ell(n+1, v(y,r))p(n,y;\,dr) \ge E_\ell(n,y)\,.$$

For the power utility functions $U(x) = x^c/c$, $0 < c \le 1$, we have for $(n,y) \in Z$:

$$(P) \qquad \int r^c E_c(n+1, v(y,r))p(n,y;\,dr) \ge c\,E_c(n,y)^2\,.$$

Now we are in the position to state our main theorem:

THEOREM 3.12. *For $2 \le t \le T$ and $(n,y) \in Z$ we have*

a) *for the logarithmic utility function $U(x) = \log x$:*
   i) $\mathcal{J}_{t-1}^a(n,y) - \mathcal{J}_t^a(n,y) \ge \mathcal{J}_t^a(n,y) - \mathcal{J}_{t+1}^a(n,y)\,, a = 1,2\,,$
   ii) $\mathcal{J}_{t-1}(n,y) - \mathcal{J}_t(n,y) \ge \mathcal{J}_t(n,y) - \mathcal{J}_{t+1}(n,y)\,,$

b) *for the power utility functions $U(x) = x^c/c$, $0 < c \le 1$:*
   i) $\mathcal{J}_{t-1}^a(n,y) - s^c\mathcal{J}_t^a(n,y) \ge \mathcal{J}_t^a(n,y) - s^c\mathcal{J}_{t+1}^a(n,y)$, $a = 1,2$,
   ii) $\mathcal{J}_{t-1}(n,y) - s^c\mathcal{J}_t(n,y) \ge \mathcal{J}_t(n,y) - s^c\mathcal{J}_{t+1}(n,y)$.

PROOF. *We prove only part b), because it is more ambitious than a). But the proof of part a) goes in a similar manner.*

The proof is made by simultaneous backward induction over i) and ii).

1) *Let $t = T$ and $\mathcal{J}_{T+1}^1(n,y) = \mathcal{J}_{T+1}^2(n,y) = 1/c$.*

i) α)*Let* $a = 1$.

$$\begin{aligned}\mathcal{J}^1_{T-1}(n,y) - s^c \mathcal{J}^1_T(n,y) &\geq s^c \mathcal{J}^1_T(n,y) - s^c \mathcal{J}^1_T(n,y) = 0 \\ &= \mathcal{J}^1_T(n,y) - s^c \mathcal{J}^1_{T+1}(n,y)\,.\end{aligned}$$

β) *Let* $a = 2$ *and* $d_T(n,y) < 0$.

$$\begin{aligned}\mathcal{J}^2_{T-1}(n,y) - s^c \mathcal{J}^2_T(n,y) &\geq \int r^c \mathcal{J}^1_T(n+1, v(y,r)) p(n,y;\, dr) \\ &\quad - s^c E_c(n,y) = 0 \\ &> E_c(n,y) - s^c/c \\ &= \mathcal{J}^2_T(n,y) - s^c \mathcal{J}^2_{T+1}(n,y)\,.\end{aligned}$$

γ) *Let* $a = 2$ *and* $d_T(n,y) \geq 0$.

$$\begin{aligned}\mathcal{J}^2_{T-1}(n,y) - s^c \mathcal{J}^2_T(n,y) &\geq \int r^c E_c(n+1, v(y,r)) p(n,y;\, dr) \\ &\quad - s^c E_c(n,y) \\ &\geq c E_c(n,y)^2 - s^c E_c(n,y) \\ &= c E_c(n,y)(E_c(n,y) - s^c/c) \\ &\geq E_c(n,y) - s^c/c \\ &= \mathcal{J}^2_T(n,y) - s^c \mathcal{J}^2_{T+1}(n,y)\,.\end{aligned}$$

The second inequality holds because of (P) *whereas the third one is true because of* $s \geq 1$. *As* $d_T(n,y) \geq 0$ *we have* $cE_c(n,y) \geq s^c \geq 1$.

ii)

$$\begin{aligned}\mathcal{J}_{T-1}(n,y) + s^c \mathcal{J}_{T+1}(n,y) &\geq \max_{a=1,2}\{\mathcal{J}^a_{T-1}(n,y) + s^c \mathcal{J}^a_{T+1}(n,y)\} \\ &\geq (1+s^c) \max\{\mathcal{J}^1_T(n,y)\,,\mathcal{J}^2_T(n,y)\} \\ &= (1+s^c)\mathcal{J}_T(n,y)\,.\end{aligned}$$

2) *Let the assertions i) and ii) be true for* $t+1 \leq \tau \leq T$. *Then we have at stage* t

i) for $a = 2$:

$$
\begin{aligned}
&\mathcal{J}_{t-1}^2(n,y) - s^c \mathcal{J}_t^2(n,y) \\
&= \int r^c \left[\mathcal{J}_t(n+1, v(y,r)) - s^c \mathcal{J}_{t+1}(n+1, v(y,r))\right] p(n,y;\, dr) \\
&\geq \int r^c \left[\mathcal{J}_{t+1}(n+1, v(y,r)) - s^c \mathcal{J}_{t+2}(n+1, v(y,r))\right] p(n,y;\, dr) \\
&= \mathcal{J}_t^2(n,y) - s^c \mathcal{J}_{t+1}^2(n,y) \,.
\end{aligned}
$$

ii) is proved like 1) ii).

Now we have to pose the question when the assumptions (L) and (P), respectively, are fulfilled.

First we present general conditions for the validity of (P).

LEMMA 3.13. *Let for $(n,y) \in Z$ and let for a power utility function $U(x) = x^c/c$, $0 < c \leq 1$,*

a) *$r \to r^c\, E_c(n+1, v(y,r))$ be convex, and*
b) *$E_c(n+1, v(y, E_1(n,y))) \geq E_c(n,y)$.*

Then (P) holds.

PROOF.

$$
\begin{aligned}
&\int r^c E_c(n+1, v(y,r)) p(n,y;\, dr) \\
&\geq c E_c(n,y) E_c(n+1, v(y, E_1(n,y))) \\
&\geq c E_c(n,y)^2 \,.
\end{aligned}
$$

The validity of the first inequality results from a) be means of Jensen's inequality.

COROLLARY 3.14. *Let the utility function of final wealth be linear, i.e. $U(x) = x$. Furthermore, let the return r of the risky asset B be $G(\alpha,\theta)$–distributed and let the prior distribution $\overline{\mu}$ for the unknown parameter θ be the conjugate $G(\gamma,\delta)$–distribution.*

Then (P) holds.

PROOF. *For $(n,y) \in Z$ the posterior distribution $p(n,y;.)$ of the return of the risky asset B is a Pearson–type–VI–distribution (see Table 2.2); therefore, we have*

$$E_1(n,y) = \alpha(\delta + y)/(n\alpha + \gamma - 1)\ , \quad \gamma > \max\{0, 1-(L+1)\alpha\}\,.$$

As we assumed a linear utility function, i.e. $c = 1$, assumption a) of Lemma 3.13 is satisfied.

Furthermore, we have:

$$\begin{aligned} E_1(n+1, y + E_1(n,y)) &= \alpha[\delta + y + E_1(n,y)]/[(n+1)\alpha + \gamma - 1] \\ &= E_1(n,y)\,. \end{aligned}$$

So assumption b) of Lemma 3.13 also is fulfilled and thus (P) holds.

LEMMA 3.15. *Let the utility function of final wealth be logarithmic, i.e. $U(x) = \log x$.*

Furthermore, let the return r of the risky asset B be $LN(\theta, \sigma^2)$– distributed and let the prior distribution $\overline{\mu}$ of the unknown parameter θ be the conjugate $N(\mu, \tau^2)$–distribution.

Then (L) holds.

PROOF. *For $(n,y) \in Z$ the posterior return distribution $p(n,y;.)$ of the risky asset B is also a Lognormal distribution (see Table 2.2); therefore, we have:*

$$E_\ell(n,y) = \mu_\ell(n,y) = (\tau^2 y + \sigma^2 \mu)/(\tau^2 n + \sigma^2)\,.$$

Furthermore

$$\int E_\ell(n+1, yr)p(n,y;\, dr) = E_\ell(n,y)$$

and thus (L) is satisfied.

We show in the following that assumptions (P) and (L) are always fulfilled if the return distribution of the risky asset B is a two–point distribution.

LEMMA 3.16. *Let the return distribution ν_θ of the risky asset B be a two–point distribution with values $r1 > r2 \geq 0$ and $\nu_\theta(\{r1\}) = \theta$ and let*

$\overline{\mu}$ be any non–degenerate prior distribution over the unit interval of the unknown parameter θ.

a) *Let the utility function of final wealth be logarithmic, i.e. $U(x) = \log x$.*
Then (L) holds.

b) *Let the utility function of final wealth be of power type, i.e. $U(x) = x^c/c$, $0 < c \leq 1$.*
Then (P) holds.

PROOF. *We show only part b). Part a) can be proved along the same lines. For $(n,y) \in Z$ we prove that*

$$(3,37)\quad \begin{aligned} &p(n,y)r1^c E_c(n+1,y+1) + [1-p(n,y)]r2^c E_c(n+1,y) \\ &\geq cE_c(n,y)^2\,, \end{aligned}$$

where $p(n,y)$ is the posterior probability by return $r1$, defined by (3,31). By means of Lemma 3.11 we have for the c–fold of the left–hand–side of (3,37):

$$\begin{aligned} &p(n,y)r1^c[p(n+1,y+1)r1^c + (1-p(n+1,y+1))r2^c] \\ &+(1-p(n,y))r2^c[p(n+1,y)r1^c + (1-p(n+1,y))r2^c] \\ &= p(n,y)p(n+1,y+1)r1^c(r1^c - r2^c) + p(n,y)r1^c r2^c \\ &+ p(n,y)r2^c(r1^c - r2^c) - p(n,y)p(n+1,y+1)r2^c(r1^c - r2^c) \\ &+(1-p(n,y))r2^{2c} \\ &= p(n,y)[p(n+1,y+1)(r1^c - r2^c)^2 + r2^c(r1^c - r2^c)] + p(n,y)r1^c r2^c \\ &+(1-p(n,y))r2^{2c} \\ &\geq p(n,y)[p(n,y)(r1^c - r2^c)^2 + r2^c(r1^c - r2^c)] + p(n,y)r1^c r2^c \\ &+(1-p(n,y))r2^{2c} \\ &= p(n,y)^2(r1^c - r2^c)^2 + 2p(n,y)r2^c(r1^c - r2^c) + r2^{2c}\,. \end{aligned}$$

The inequality is true because of the monotonicity of the posterior probability $p(n,y)$ (see Corollary 2.14).

The c–fold of the right–hand–side of (3,37) is:

$$\begin{aligned} &p(n,y)^2 r1^{2c} + 2p(n,y)(1-p(n,y))r1^c r2^c + (1-p(n,y))^2 r2^{2c} \\ =&p(n,y)^2(r1^c - r2^c)^2 + 2p(n,y)r1^c r2^c + r2^{2c} - 2p(n,y)r2^{2c}\,. \end{aligned}$$

Thus, we have shown the validity of (3,37).

The preceding theorems illustrate that Theorem 3.12 can be used in important special cases. We have not listed all such cases, but we first of all concentrated on those important for the subsequent analysis, e.g. those with a linear utility function of final wealth. Besides Corollary 3.14, assumption (P) is e.g. satisfied for the linear utility function as well as for lognormally distributed return of asset B with prior Normal distribution. This can be verified by means of Lemma 3.13.

3.2.3.1 The Stopping Rule

Theorem 3.12 enables us to prove the first structural property of the optimal binary portfolio policy, the so–called stopping rule. Such a policy is also known as a stop–loss–strategy.

THEOREM 3.17. *For* $1 \leq t \leq T-1$ *and* $(n,y) \in Z$ *we have:*

$$f_t(n,y) = 1 \quad \textit{implies} \quad f_{t+1}(n,y) = 1\,.$$

PROOF. *By definition* (3,36) *the assertion of the theorem is equivalent to*

$$\begin{aligned} d_t(n,y) < 0 \quad &\textit{implies} \quad d_{t+1}(n,y) < 0 \quad \textit{or} \\ d_{t+1}(n,y) \geq 0 \quad &\textit{implies} \quad d_t(n,y) \geq d_{t+1}(n,y)\,. \end{aligned}$$

For the latter one we have by means of Theorem 3.12 for the power utility functions $U(x) = x^c/c$, $0 < c \leq 1$:

$$\begin{aligned} d_t(n,y) &= \mathcal{J}_t^2(n,y) - \mathcal{J}_t^1(n,y) \\ &= \mathcal{J}_t^2(n,y) - s^c \mathcal{J}_{t+1}^2(n,y) \\ &\geq \mathcal{J}_{t+1}^2(n,y) - s^c \mathcal{J}_{t+2}^2(n,y) \\ &\geq \mathcal{J}_{t+1}^2(n,y) - s^c \mathcal{J}_{t+2}(n,y) \\ &= d_{t+1}(n,y)\,. \end{aligned}$$

For the interpretation of this result, recall the small investor who for the first time in his life puts part of his savings into a risky asset. More or less this behaviour can be regarded as speculation or gambling on the capital market.

If initially the returns of the risky asset B are quite high and if after some planning periods the returns are considerably low, perhaps lower than the riskless return s, as a first disappointment the investor will transfer the "risky" wealth to his savings account. This disappointment causes the investor to stay away from gambling on the capital market for a while. During that time period, expressed by the planning horizon T, he is not interested in the prices and returns of the risky asset B as well as of other risky assets. All the wealth is kept on the riskless savings account, i.e. $f_\tau(n,y) = 1$, $t+1 \leq \tau \leq T$.

In our opinion this seems to be a possible explanation to justify assumption B7, which states that investment in the riskless asset A causes no change of the information state (n,y) of the risky asset B.

But such an investment behaviour as it is expressed by the stop–loss–strategy is widely employed, not only by small investors but also by large institutions. It might be interesting to extend the analysis to the inclusion of transaction costs by switching from one asset to the other in such a way that the optimality of a stop–loss–strategy is ensured.

The stopping rule also leads to important consequences for the computation of the optimal binary portfolio policy. As the following result shows, it remains only to compute the value functions $\mathcal{J}_t^2(n,y)$.

LEMMA 3.18. *For* $1 \leq t \leq T$ *and* $(n,y) \in Z$ *we have*

a) *for the logarithmic utility function* $U(x) = \log x$*:*
  i) $f_t(n,y) = 1$ *implies*
  $\mathcal{J}_t(n,y) = \mathcal{J}_t^1(n,y) = (T+1-t)\log s$,
  ii) $\mathcal{J}_t(n,y) = \max\{(T+1-t)\log s,\ \mathcal{J}_t^2(n,y)\}$,

b) *for the power utility functions* $U(x) = x^c/c$, $0 < c \leq 1$*:*
  i) $f_t(n,y) = 1$ *implies* $\mathcal{J}_t(n,y) = \mathcal{J}_t^1(n,y) = s^{c(T+1-t)}/c$,
  ii) $\mathcal{J}_t(n,y) = \max\{s^{c(T+1-t)}/c\,,\mathcal{J}_t^2(n,y)\}$.

PROOF. *For both types of utility functions part i) is shown by induction using Theorem 3.17. Part ii) results from i) by means of Lemma 3.10.*

3.2.3.2 The Monotonicity Property

Building on the stopping rule property of the optimal binary portfolio policy, we now turn the attention to a second structural result. We show that the optimal binary investment decisions $f_t(n,y)$, $t = 1,\ldots,T$, from (3,35) are monotone functions of the information state (n,y). Starting point is the monotonicity of the value functions of dynamic programming (see Lemma 3.9).

THEOREM 3.19. *Let (n,y), $(n',y') \in Z$ with $(n,y) \leq (n',y')$ in the sense of (2,8) and (2,8'), respectively. Then we have for $1 \leq t \leq T$:*

$$f_t(n,y) = 2 \quad \textit{implies} \quad f_t(n',y') = 2\ .$$

PROOF. *We show that $f_t(n',y') = 1$ implies $f_t(n,y) = 1$, or equivalently that $d_t(n',y') < 0$ implies $d_t(n,y) < 0$. Then we have by means of Lemma 3.9, Lemma 3.18i) and Lemma 3.10 for the logarithmic utility function $U(x) = \log x$:*

$$\mathcal{J}_t^2(n,y) \leq \mathcal{J}_t^2(n',y') < \mathcal{J}_t^1(n',y') = (T-t+1)\log s \leq \mathcal{J}_t^1(n,y)\,.$$

Thus $d_t(n,y) < 0$ holds.
For the power utility functions of final wealth the proof is performed in the same way.

Recall that for two information states (n,y) and (n',y') the relation $(n,y) \leq (n',y')$ defined in (2,8) and (2,8'), respectively, says that state (n',y') contains better information than state (n,y), e.g. the equal number of observations $n = n'$ leads to a higher cumulative return y' than y. Now suppose that in planning period t the investor decides for the risky asset B given the information state (n,y), i.e. $f_t(n,y) = 2$. Then given information state (n',y') he will also invest in the risky asset B, i.e. $f_t(n',y') = 2$.

This behaviour is evident: the higher the past returns of the risky asset B, the more likely the investor puts his money into asset B.

From a geometrical view–point the monotonicity of the optimal binary investment decision functions $f_t(n,y)$ leads to the separation of the optimality regions of the two assets into two convex sets with respect to the information state (n,y).

Now suppose that at the beginning of the planning process, i.e. at the beginning of planning period one, we start with information state $(n,y) = (0,0)$ in case of the Gamma and the two–point distribution and with $(n,y) = (0,1)$ in case of the Lognormal distribution. This can be done without loss of generality because the prior information of returns of the risky asset B can be included into the prior distribution $\overline{\mu}$ of the unknown parameter θ.

Then the determination of the optimal investment decision functions f_t, $1 \leq t \leq T$, reduces to the computation of the T numbers $y_1^*, \ldots, y_T^*$, which unfortunately often is impossible in an analytical way. Because of Theorem 3.19 and Lemma 3.18, y_t^* is the solution of the following equation, and that

- for the logarithmic utility function $U(x) = \log x$:

$$\mathcal{J}_t^2(t-1, y_t^*) = (T - t + 1)\log s\,,$$

- for the power utility functions $U(x) = x^c/c$, $0 < c \leq 1$:

$$\mathcal{J}_t^2(t-1, y_t^*) = s^{c(T-t+1)}/c\,.$$

For the definition of y_t^* in the case of the discrete two–point distribution we refer to section 3.2.5.

As a consequence we can simplify the optimal investment decision functions:

$$\overline{f}_t(y) := f_t(t-1, y) = \begin{cases} 1 & y < y_t^* \\ 2 & y \geq y_t^*\,. \end{cases} \qquad (3{,}38)$$

The numbers y_t^*, $1 \leq t \leq T$, are termed as control limits. The optimal binary portfolio policy is a so–called control–limit–policy. Its interpretation is as follows:

If in planning period t the cumulative return y, which during the first $t-1$ planning periods has been earned by investment in the risky asset B(stopping rule!), is not smaller than y_t^*, then in this period it is optimal to put all the initial wealth into asset B, i.e. $\overline{f}_t(y) = 2$.

The actual computation of the control limits $y_1^*, \ldots, y_T^*$ causes big problems and often can only be performed numerically, even in the case of conjugate return and prior distributions of the risky asset B.

Thus, we later on develop an algorithm only for the two–point return distribution with Beta prior distribution to compute the optimal binary portfolio policy. Additionally, this algorithm uses the "stay–on–a–winner–property" which we prove next.

3.2.3.3 The Stay–on–a–Winner–Property

In this section we assume the return distribution of the risky asset B to be a two–point distribution. We show for this special case of the binary dynamic portfolio model that the so–called "stay–on–a–winner–property" holds which has its name from the one–armed bandit models. In marketing this property can be interpreted as brand loyality.

THEOREM 3.20. *Let the distribution of the return of the risky asset B be a two-point distribution. For $1 \le t \le T-1$ and $(n,y) \in Z$ then we have:*

$$f_t(n,y) = 2 \quad \textit{implies} \quad f_{t+1}(n+1, y+1) = 2\,.$$

PROOF.
We show that $d_{t+1}(n+1, y+1) < 0$ implies $d_t(n,y) \le d_{t+1}(n,y)$. By means of Theorem 3.19 we conclude that $d_{t+1}(n+1,y+1) < 0$ implies $d_{t+1}(n+1,y) < 0$ and $d_{t+1}(n,y) < 0$.

Using Theorem 3.17 we then have:

$$d_\tau(n,y) < 0\,,\ d_\tau(n+1,y+1) < 0\,,\ d_\tau(n+1,y) < 0 \quad \textit{for} \quad t+2 \le \tau \le T\,.$$

Therefore, by means of Lemma 3.18i) and assumption B3, i.e. $s \ge 1$, we have for the power utility functions $U(x) = x^c/c$, $0 < c \le 1$:

$$\begin{aligned} d_t(n,y) &= \mathcal{J}_t^2(n,y) - \mathcal{J}_t^1(n,y) \\ &= p(n,y) r1^c \mathcal{J}_{t+1}(n+1,y+1) + (1-p(n,y)) r2^c \\ &\qquad \cdot \mathcal{J}_{t+1}(n+1,y) - s^c \mathcal{J}_{t+1}(n,y) \\ &= E_c(n,y) s^{c(T-t)} - s^{c(T-t+1)}/c \\ &= s^{c(T-t)}(E_c(n,y) - s^c/c) \\ &\le s^{c(T-t-1)}(E_c(n,y) - s^c/c) \\ &= p(n,y) r1^c s^{c(T-t-1)}/c \\ &\qquad + (1-p(n,y)) r2^c s^{c(T-t-1)}/c - s^{c(T-t)}/c \\ &= \mathcal{J}_{t+1}^2(n,y) - \mathcal{J}_{t+1}^1(n,y) \\ &= d_{t+1}(n,y)\,. \end{aligned}$$

If in planning period t given information state (n,y) the investor decides for the risky asset B, i.e. $f_t(n,y) = 2$, and if in that planning period he obtains the high return $r1$, then in the subsequent planning period $t+1$ he will also invest in the risky asset B. In such a situation it is optimal not to change the investment behaviour — it pays to stay on the "winning" asset B. But if the low return $r2$ is obtained it is not possible to make an assertion about the investment behaviour of the following planning period.

3.2.4. Remarks on the Implementation of the Model

We are not dealing here with numerical problems of computing the optimal portfolio policy (3,38). Instead we briefly discuss the consequences of the structural properties for the practical implementation of the model. The crucial property certainly is the stopping rule; an investment policy of this type is usually called "partial myopic" (cp. Mossin (1968)).

Given the past returns of the risky asset B and his subjective beliefs, suppose in the first planning period the optimal decision for the investor in the (unique) information state $(0,0)$ and $(0,1)$, respectively, is to keep all his money on the savings account, i.e. to invest in the riskless asset A. Due to the stopping rule in all succeeding planning periods up to the planning horizon it is also optimal to invest in the riskless asset A.

But this does not mean that the investor has to wait T planning periods before he again can try to put part of his money into a risky asset. No, the can pursue a kind of rolling horizon method: If the previous situation prevails, the investor looks at the next planning period as the new beginning of the planning process. Based on the revised information he decides whether it is then optimal to invest in the risky asset. In prinicple this rolling horizon procedure can be repeated to any extent desired. But it seems reasonable either to stop after a certain number of trials or to continue the procedure with another risky asset than B.

If in the first planning period it is optimal to invest in the risky asset B, this investment behaviour has to be continued until either the stopping rule prescribes the riskless asset A or the planning horizon T is reached. Then the investor can act according to the previously sketched method of rolling horizon.

3.2.5 Sensitivity Analyses

Now we use the structural properties of the optimal binary portfolio policy for constructing an algorithm in the case the return distribution of the risky asset B is a two–point distribution. For that purpose we show first that the control limits y_t^* defined in (3,38) are nondecreasing with respect to t.

By means of this algorithm we perform several numerical sensitivity investigations for the case that the unknown parameter θ, i.e. the probability of the high return $r1$, a priori is Beta–distributed. Special interest is placed on the changes of the optimal investment decisions if, on the one hand, the utility function of final wealth is varied and if, on the other hand, the prior distribution is varied with respect to its variance and skewness.

Furthermore, we investigate the influence of a variation of the planning horizon on the optimal portfolio policy.

3.2.5.1 An Algorithm for the Two–Point–Return Distribution

As described in section 3.2.3.2, we now assume that at the beginning of the first planning period the information state is $(n, y) = (0, 0)$. Thus, in each planning period t, $1 \leq t \leq T$, only t information states are possible; we put them together in the set Z_t:

$$Z_t := \{(t-1, 0), \ldots, (t-1, t-1)\}.$$

The control limits y_t^* are in the case of the discrete two–point distribution defined as follows

- for the logarithmic utility function $U(x) = \log x$:
  $y_t^* = \min\{y | \mathcal{J}_t^2(t-1, y) \geq (T-t+1) \log s\,, (t-1, y) \in Z_t\}$,
- for the power utility functions $U(x) = x^c/c$, $0 < c \leq 1$:
  $y_t^* = \min\{y | \mathcal{J}_t^2(t-1, y) \geq s^{c(T-t+1)}/c\,, (t-1, y) \in Z_t\}$.

If in planning period t in each of the information states from the set Z_t it is optimal to invest in the riskless asset A, we agree upon $y_t^* = t$.

Before stating the algorithm we show a monotonicity property of the control limits y_t^* from (3,38) thereby considerably reducing the computational requirements.

LEMMA 3.21. *For $1 \leq t \leq T-1$ we have for the control limits of the optimal binary portfolio policy defined by* (3,38):

$$y_t^* \leq y_{t+1}^*.$$

PROOF. *Because of $f_{t+1}(t, y_{t+1}^*) = 2$ we have by means of Theorem 3.17 — the stopping rule — also $f_t(t, y_{t+1}^*) = 2$.*

The monotonicity of the optimal investment decision functions then implies $f_t(t-1, y_{t+1}^*) = 2$ and thus $y_t^* \leq y_{t+1}^*$.

An algorithm for the computation of the optimal portfolio policy in case of the logarithmic utility function $U(x) = \log x$:

1. Let $t = T$ and $y_{T+1}^* = T - 1$.

2. Let $y = y^*_{t+1}$ and $n = t - 1$.
3. Compute $p(n,y)$ and $\mathcal{J}^2_t(n,y)$.
4. If $\mathcal{J}^2_t(n,y) \geq (T-n)\log s$, then let $\mathcal{J}_t(n,y) = \mathcal{J}^2_t(n,y)$ and $y = y-1$ and go to 6.
5. Otherwise let $y^*_t = y + 1$ and $\mathcal{J}_t(n,z) = (T - n)\log s$ for $z = y, y-1, \ldots, 0$ and go to 8.
6. If $y \geq 0$ then go to 3.
7. Otherwise let $y^*_t = 0$.
8. Let $t = t - 1$.
9. If $t > 0$ go to 2.
10. Otherwise STOP.

In case of the power utility functions x^c/c, in steps 4 and 5 $(T-n)\log s$ has to be replaced by $s^{c(T-n)}/c$, $0 < c \leq 1$.

3.2.5.2 Variation of the Utility Function

We are dealing with the following question: What is the effect of a change of the utility function and thus of the coefficient of absolute risk aversion on the optimal portfolio policy? The prior distribution of the unknown probability θ of the high return $r1$ of the risky asset B is in the following always the Beta–$B(\gamma,\delta)$–distribution. Given $(n,y) \in Z$ we have from Table 2.2 $p(n,y) = (\gamma + y)/(\gamma + \delta + n)$.

In this section we assume $\gamma = \delta$, which means that the prior distribution is symmetric.

For matter of comparison we choose the following reference model:

$$T = 10,\ \ s = 1.05,\ \ r1 = 1.15,\ \ r2 = 1, \gamma = \delta = 2, c = 1\,.$$

As $c = 1$, the investor is assumed to be risk neutral with respect to utility, i.e. $U(x) = x$. The optimal portfolio policy for the reference model is

t	1	2	3	4	5	6	7	8	9	10
y^*_t	0	0	0	0	1	1	1	2	2	3

This means that in the first four planning periods in each possible information state from Z_t, $1 \leq t \leq 4$, the optimal investment decision is the risky asset B. Up to the last planning period $t = 10$ the high return must have been obtained at least three times in order that it is optimal to invest once again in the risky asset B.

Now we vary the coefficient of risk aversion $c, 0 < c \leq 1$. Increasing risk aversion is achieved by a decrease of c; in particular we want to remember that $U(x) = \log x$ can be looked upon as limiting function of x^c/c as c goes to zero with respect to absolute risk aversion.

	Planning Period t									
c	1	2	3	4	5	6	7	8	9	10
0.8	0	0	0	0	1	1	2	2	2	3
0.1	0	0	0	0	1	1	2	2	3	3
0	0	0	0	0	1	1	2	2	3	3

Table 3.1: Control limits y_t^* for several coefficients of risk aversion.

The comparison of Table 3.1 with the optimal policy of the reference model shows almost no variation of the optimal investment decisions: The optimal behaviour of the risk neutral investor scarcely differs from that of the "square–root"–investor or from that of the logarithmic investor. In particular the optimal portfolio policy does not change at all if c lies between 0.2 and 0.8.

The summary of these numerical investigations: The optimal binary portfolio policy is almost insensitive to variation of the utility functions in the range from logarithmic to linear.

3.2.5.3 Variation of the Prior Distribution

In the following we always assume that the investor is risk neutral with respect to utility function, i.e. $c = 1$. The prior expected return of asset B is as in the preceding section $E_1(0,0) = 1.075$, which means that the prior distribution is still symmetric ($\gamma = \delta$). The variance of the prior Beta distribution decreases as the parameters γ and δ are increased. The variance of the reference model, i.e. $\gamma = \delta = 2$, is 0.05. A quarter of this variance, already achieved by specifying $\gamma = \delta = 9$, has the effect that in each planning period it is optimal to invest in each possible information state in the risky asset B. In this case we have $y_t^* = 0$, $1 \leq t \leq 10$.

The same portfolio policy is optimal if compared to the reference model the high return $r1$ is raised from 1.15 to 1.4.

Now we abandon the symmetry of the prior distribution and consider instead distributions with positive skewness. A Beta distribution is positively skewed if parameter δ is larger than parameter γ.

From Table 3.1 we have seen that a symmetric prior distribution leads to almost no change of the optimal portfolio policy if the coefficient of risk aversion c, $0 < c \leq 1$, is varied. Now we pose the opposite question: What changes of the optimal investment policy result from the variation of the (positive) skewness of the prior distribution, given a linear utility function ?

The succeeding Table 3.2 presents the optimal control limits y_t^* for different values of the parameters γ and δ, but always the same prior expected return of asset B $E_1(0,0) = 1.06$. The γ- δ-values are arranged in such a way that the skewness as well as (unfortunately) the variance of the prior distribution are decreasing. Because we have already fixed the expected value, it is not possible to keep the variance constant and at the same time to vary the skewness — the Beta distribution is only characterized by two parameters.

γ	δ	Skewness	Variance	1	2	3	4	5	6	7	8	9	10
1	1.5	0.34	0.07	0	0	1	1	1	2	2	2	3	3
2	3	0.29	0.04	0	0	0	1	1	1	2	2	3	3
4	6	0.23	0.022	0	0	0	0	1	1	1	2	2	3
6	9	0.19	0.019	0	0	0	0	0	1	1	2	2	2

Table 3.2: Control limits y_t^* by variation of the skewness and the variance of the prior distribution.

A first glance at Table 3.2 shows familiar results: Larger γ-δ- values, which are equivalent to smaller skewness and smaller variance, cause a more risky investment behaviour, represented by smaller control limits y_t^*.

Of special interest is, of course, the comparison of the optimal portfolio policies for symmetric prior distributions — the reference model and Table 3.1 — with those for skewed prior distributions given by Table 3.2.

First we compare the last row of Table 3.1, representing the optimal portfolio policy of an investor with logarithmic utility function of final wealth, with the second row of Table 3.2, where against the reference model just parameter δ is set equal to 3. The latter case shows a little more cautious investment behaviour than that of the logarithmic investor.

In other words: A slight modification of the parameters of the prior Beta distribution compared to those of the reference model, and that in the direction of positive skewness, leads to a more risk averse portfolio policy than that expressed by the utility function with the largest coefficient of absolute risk aversion, namely the logarithmic utility function.

Additionally the variance in the former case 0.04 is less than the variance 0.05 of the reference model.

What conclusions can be drawn from the numerical results of Table 3.1 and Table 3.2 ? Whereas the variation of the coefficient c of absolute risk aversion of the utility function results in almost no changes of the optimal investment behaviour, the optimal portfolio policy reacts rather sensitive to variations of the prior distribution.

In our opinion this result seems to be a moderate indication for the suggestion to express the risk attitudes of an investor not only by a strictly concave utility function but also more often by the (positive) skewness of the probability distributions involved.

3.2.5.4 Variation of the Planning Horizon

The goal in the binary Bayesian dynamic portfolio model is the maximization of the expected utility of wealth at the (finite) planning horizon T. This kind of decision model raises, of course, the question, how robust the optimal portfolio policy is with respect to variations of the planning horizon T.

For an answer let us briefly return to our reference model with the planning horizon $T = 10$. Assume that due to the realized returns in all 10 planning periods it is optimal to invest in the risky asset B and that the investor wants to continue this policy in the future. Thus, with the intention to increase the planning horizon, he clearly poses the question: Instead of 10, I want to invest over 20 planning periods in the risky asset B. Has the investment behaviour during the first 10 planning periods been optimal if the planning horizon T is 20 periods ?

We can calm the investor, at least in numerical sense. The computations lead to the following assertion:

$$T_1 < T_2 \quad \text{implies} \quad y_t^{*1} \geq y_t^{*2} \quad \text{for} \quad 1 \leq t \leq T_1 .$$

The longer the planning horizon T, the more is the investor willing to put his money into the risky asset B. Because the optimal investment decisions are not myopic, the investor appreciates a long planning horizon as long learning process with respect to the return distribution of the risky asset B.

Finally we want to investigate whether there exists a so–called "turnpike horizon" T^*. The turnpike horizon T^* is defined as the smallest planning horizon for which all portfolio models with longer planning horizon than T^* have the same optimal investment decisions during the first T^* planning periods.

The numerical investigations, however, show that the optimal portfolio policies for different planning horizons are quite similar but that no turnpike horizon exists.

3.2.6 Conclusions

The preceding section on numerical sensitivity analyses shows that risk averse behaviour of an investor can be expressed not only by the choice of a strictly concave utility function but also apparently by the specification of the return distribution of the risky asset B.

But the suggested procedure, namely a linear utility function together with a return distribution with positive skewness, is of no use in "classic" dynamic portfolio analysis. There first of all the determination of an optimal diversified portfolio is of interest, which in general is composed of more than one asset.

As is well known this is achieved by specifying a strictly concave utility function provided the investor is risk averse. Besides from a risk averse utility function in classic dynamic portfolio analysis usually a symmetric distribution of the returns is assumed, as we have already discussed earlier.

Therefore, a suggestion for investors who are interested in portfolios consisting of more than one asset: Depart from the often made assumption of a logarithmic utility function and normally distributed returns; use a model with also logarithmic utility function of final wealth; but allow not only symmetric return distributions.

Finally to this chapter once again we deal with the structural properties of the binary dynamic portfolio model, i.e. the stopping rule, the control–limit–property, and in case of the two–point return distribution the stay–on–a–winner–property. We have already mentioned earlier empirical investigations saying that in practice almost no investor owns an optimal diversified portfolio. Instead many investors behave according to simple strategies like e.g. the stop–loss–strategy which in the binary portfolio model is characterized by the stopping rule.

This kind of investment behaviour evidently is practised not only by small investors but also by large financial institutions. Moreover, the structural properties enable plausible interpretations thereby additionally documenting their importance.

All in all we can say that the aim should be a reasonable coexistence of, on the one hand, classic dynamic portfolio analysis and, on the other hand, binary dynamic portfolio models.

4. The Optimal Timing of Investment

In the previous chapter we have only been dealing with the behaviour of private investors. In this part of the work the main interest is devoted to the analysis of the investment decisions of a firm. We concentrate on the investment in real, i.e. productive, assets, which are the means of producing consumption goods. In the final part of this chapter we consider again a private investor who wants to put his money in a financial asset.

We are not concerned with the choice among several investment projects. Instead we determine the optimal timing of an already selected project. Thereby also the question is included whether it should be invested or not at all. Thus, we assume that the total set of investment projects available to the firm has already been defined (cp. e.g. Haley/Schall (1979), pp. 47).

Usually an investment project is composed of several dependent parts (modules). The alternatives, i.e. combinations of modules, within a project are mutually exclusive. Clearly, one alternative is to reject the project. Static investment analysis says to choose the "best" among all current alternatives of a project (cp. Haley/Schall (1979), p. 49).

But for some investment projects it is not only necessary to consider current alternatives but also future alternatives. This dynamic aspect, the question when to invest in a project, is not paid much attention in traditional investment analysis; it is of no importance for reversible projects. If the investment project is a real asset which is at least irreversible in fact, e.g. a machine–plant, it is also decisive to determine at what point of time to undertake the project.

Irreversibility implies that a positive net present value (NPV) or market value of the project is only a necessary but not a sufficient condition for the decision to invest. Assume that the irreversible project consists of one module, which means it is indivisible. Then the only two current alternatives are to accept or to postpone the project. In future the investor is confronted with the same pair of alternatives. At the time horizon again one alternative is to accept the project, the other one is to reject it. Therefore, the decision to accept the project at time t_1 and the decision to accept the project at t_2 are mutually exclusive alternatives. If the investor decides to accept the project at t_1, it is impossible to undertake it at a later point of time t_2.

We shall show later on that this opportunity or option to undertake the project at a future point of time is represented by a positive value, the option value. If at some point of time the NPV or market value minus capital cost exceeds this option value, then it is optimal to accept the investment project.

Thus, the usual NPV–rule is not enough for the decision whether to accept or not an irreversible project (cp. for the deterministic case Marglin (1967), chapter 2, and for the stochastic case e.g. Baldwin/Meyer (1979), Bernanke (1983)).

In this chapter we study the optimal timing of investment under conditions of uncertainty in an irreversible real asset, e.g. a machine, by using a discrete–time model. Contrary to Roberts/Weitzman (1981) who consider *R&D* projects, we are dealing with investment projects which are traded on the capital markets. Thus, in every planning period we are able to determine a unique market value for the project whose expected value is used as decision criterion whether to invest and if yes, when to invest (for the justification of this objective function also under conditions of uncertainty, cp. Wilhelm (1983)).

In each planning period the probability distribution of the market value is revised according to the Bayesian law. Furthermore, we consider the possibility that there does not exist an opportunity for investing in each planning period. The probability of an investment opportunity is assumed to be unkown a priori and is also updated period by period in a Bayesian manner.

Like in the dynamic portfolio model of the previous chapter, we also show that the optimal investment policy possesses several economically appealing features. Moreover, we perform extensive sensitivity analyses thereby comparing our results with those of already known models.

Finally, we motivate that this type of model cannot only be used for the investment analysis of real assets but also seems to be suitable for a class of financial assets. Assuming that the option cannot be sold on the secondary market and that the exercise price is not invested at the riskless rate of return, we can determine the optimal exercise date of an American call option with this model. This is a call option which can be exercised up to a specified point of time, the expiration date.

Before we discuss this model under conditions of uncertainty in detail, first we briefly sketch the difference between reversible and irreversible projects from the point of view of investment analysis. In the sequel we introduce some models for the determination of the optimal investment date under conditions of certainty and under conditions of risk. We first of all focus on those properties of the optimal investment policy allowing the comparison with results of the model under conditions of uncertainty.

4.1 Investment Decisions and the Economic Life of Projects

The investment program of a corporate firm, of course, has to be coordinated with the preferences and tastes of its shareholders. When we assume that all economic decisions can be reduced to questions about consumption, the firm's objective to maximize the wealth of its shareholders is equivalent to the maximization of their (expected) utility gained from consumption over the planning horizon.

But the question is how the firm can achieve this goal to maximize its shareholders' wealth: In general it is impossible to compare and to combine individual utility functions.

Let us state the following assumptions:

- There are no barriers preventing access to the captial market and all participants act as price–takers.
- The capital markets are frictionless, i.e. there is no difference between the borrowing rate and the lending rate. The common riskless interest rate is assumed to be constant over the planning horizon and will be called the market interest rate m.

The two assumptions constitute a perfect capital market under certainty, i.e. a frictionless and perfectly competitive market (c.p. Copeland/ Weston (1983), pp. 123).

In a perfect capital market the decisions of the managers of the firm which maximize the price of the firm's shares also maximize the utility of each shareholder. Therefore, the firm's shareholders can delegate investment decisions to their managers.

This separation of investment decisions of firms from the preferences and tastes of the shareholders is known as the Fisher separation principle (cp. e.g. Brealey/Myers (1981), p. 21, Copeland/Weston (1983), pp. 18 and p. 124).

We define an investment project to consist of several, perhaps dependent modules. In this way any two investment projects of the firm are economically independent (cp. Haley/Schall (1979), pp. 47).

The only static investment decision rule under conditions of certainty which is consistent with the objective of shareholder wealth maximization is the net present value (NPV) (cp. Copeland/Weston (1983), pp. 25).

We consider an indivisible project with an economic life of T planning periods. The indivisibility guarantees that the investment project cannot be undertaken in parts. When we denote the net cash flows by $c_0, \ldots, c_T$, the net present value of the project in dependence of the discount factor $\beta := 1/(1+m)$ is given by:

$$(4,1) \qquad K(\beta) = \sum_{t=0}^{T} \beta^t c_t .$$

An investment project is called simple if the net cash flows $c_0, \ldots, c_T$ have only one change in sign. In this case the NPV given bei (4,1) typically is a nondecreasing function of the discount factor β and therefore a nonincreasing function of the market interest rate m. The reason for this latter property is that later appearing cash flows are discounted lower.

An investment project is accepted according to the NPV–rule if for given market interest rate m $K(\beta) \geq 0$ holds.

It is obvious that especially positive cash flows of a project, i.e. the benefits, are time–dependent quantities. On the one hand, they are dependent on calendar time, caused by changes over time in the demands for the goods which are produced by means of the project. On the other hand, cash flows are also influenced by the project age (cp. e.g. Marglin (1967), pp. 9).

In view of this influence of calendar time on benefits it is not only necessary to decide whether to undertake a project but also <u>when</u> to undertake it. This dynamic aspect of postponing the construction is important for those projects which may be characterized by having <u>time–dependent transaction costs</u>. For example, when an old machine has worn out and has to be replaced by a new one or when no marketing campaign is underway, the opportunity costs of reallocating resources are low. In contrast, a just installed machine or a just begun advertising activity is usually connected with high opportunity costs for disinvesting the project. Investment projects of this type tie up personnel of a firm and its other resources in long terms (cp. Baldwin/Meyer (1979), pp. 348).

Investment projects with time–dependent transactions costs may not be confused with <u>irreversible</u> projects. The examples mentioned above are not types of projects which are irreversible in principle, — a machine can be pulled down, a marketing campaign can be stopped. But usually the transaction costs are decreasing over time. Thus, it does not pay to disinvest such projects before the end of their economic lives — the projects are irreversible in fact (cp. Baldwin/Meyer (1979), pp. 350).

Due to its indivisibility the investment project is mutually exclusive over time. If the project is undertaken in a planning period, it is no more possible to invest in the project in one of the following periods. Of course, this property is not inherent to all investment projects. Especially in case of *R&D* projects often new possibilities occur for future opportunities, e.g. the utilization of patents.

The conclusion: For the type of investment projects considered it is not enough to check at one point of time whether the project has a positive NPV. Instead, in a dynamic framework we have to determine the maximal NPV discounted to the beginning of the decision process and therefore the optimal construction date. In other words: In contrast to reversible projects, the investment in irreversible projects requires that the NPV discounted to the beginning of the decision process must exceed a positive number, the so–called NPV–premium. Thus, reversible projects are more frequently undertaken than irreversible ones.

We begin with a deterministic model with time–dependent cash flows in continuous time.

4.2 A Deterministic Model in Continuous Time

We start the expedition for the determination of the optimal construction date of an irreversible real asset with a deterministic model formulated in continuous time. We use this kind of exposition in order to present the model largely in its original version which can be found in the second chapter of the book of Marglin (1967).

First of all we put together the essential assumptions to the model:

C1. There are no taxes and transaction costs. The investment project is indivisible and as already stated independent of the other projects of the firm.

C2. The economic life T of the project is assumed to be known.

C3. The riskless rate of return m of a planning period is constant over the whole planning horizon. For frictionless capital markets m is equivalent to the market interest rate (see section 4.1). It is then the market–determined opportunity cost of capital.

C4. The capital cost C are constant over the planning horizon. C is the project's initial cash outlay.

C5. We operate in continuous time.

C6. The deterministic net cash flows at a point of time depend on the calendar time as well as on the existing life of the project. Let t denote calendar time and τ the investment date, then the net cash flows $c(t, t-\tau)$ are of the following form:

$$c(t, t-\tau) = x(t) \cdot a(t-\tau)\,. \tag{4,2}$$

The function $x(t)$ represents the calendar time component. If the project is used to produce a good, then $x(t)$ is the profit per unit which first of all is determined by its given market price. x is assumed to be a monotonuous function.

The project age is considered through the component $a(t-\tau)$. It can be interpreted as the quantity of the output of the project per unit of time. The function a is assumed to be concave; furthermore $a(0) = 0$.

The NPV $K(\tau, m)$ of a project that is undertaken at time τ and whose net cash flows are given by (4,2) is:

$$K(\tau, m) = \int_{\tau}^{\tau+T} x(t) \cdot a(t-\tau) \cdot e^{-mt}\, dt - C \cdot e^{-m\tau}\,. \tag{4,3}$$

As m is the market interest rate of a planning period, in (4,3) the continuous rate of return $m_c = \log(1+m)$ had to be used in order to be correct. But for small values of the period rate of return m there is almost no difference between m and m_c. For that reason we use the approximate NPV by replacing m_c by m.

In order to reduce the computational amount, we assume for the following that the economic life of the project is "large". This is reasonable for the type of projects considered, namely irreversible real assets (cp. Swoboda (1977), p. 50). If $T \to \infty$, we obtain from (4,3):

$$K(\tau, m) = \int_{\tau}^{\infty} x(t) \cdot a(t-\tau) \cdot e^{-mt}\, dt - C \cdot e^{-m\tau}\,. \tag{4,4}$$

For the moment we consider the market interest rate m to be constant according to assumption C3. Furthermore, let the functions a and x be twice continuously differentiable. In this case the determination of the optimal construction date τ^* reduces itself to the computation of the maximal value of the NPV–function (4,4) with respect to τ.

Before employing the first order condition, we change the variables in (4,4) by defining $s = t - \tau$. Rearranging the resulting terms, we finally arrive at the following necessary optimality condition (Marglin (1967), pp. 18):

$$(4,5) \qquad -\int_{\tau^*}^{\infty} [x'(t) - mx(t)]e^{-mt}a(t-\tau^*)\,dt = mCe^{-m\tau^*}.$$

If the second order condition

$$(4,6) \qquad \int_{\tau^*}^{\infty} [x''(t) - mx'(t)]e^{-mt}a(t-\tau^*)\,dt < 0$$

is satisfied, τ^* in fact is the optimal investment date, i.e. it is the construction date which maximizes the NPV defined in (4,4).

The optimality condition (4,5) says: It is optimal to invest in the project at time τ^* if and only if the marginal losses in the net cash flows equal the marginal savings in the capital cost. The latter fact is expressed by the r.h.s. of equation (4,5), namely by the discounted interest benefits mC arising if the amount C is invested at the rate m for an infinitesimal unit of time.

The l.h.s. of the optimality condition expresses the discounted marginal losses of the net cash flows over the whole life of the investment project. The term in brackets is the difference of the marginal profit per unit $x'(t)$ and the interest cost $mx(t)$ per unit produced. $mx(t)$ has to be paid for the following reason: Assume the construction date τ^* is postponed by an infinitesimal unit of time. In order to maintain financial equilibrium it is necessary to raise a credit $x(t)$ per produced and sold unit. This expression has to be multiplied with the number of units produced $a(t-\tau^*)$.

The fairly general second order condition makes it impossible to identify classes of functions a and x such that (4,6) is satisfied which guarantees that the solution of (4,5) indeed is the NPV–maximizing construction date τ^*.

4.2.1 Net Cash Flows Independent of Project Age

In order to get a better insight to the results we simplify assumption C6. We suppose that at time t the deterministic net cash flows $c(t, t-\tau)$ depend no longer on the existing life $t - \tau$ of the project.

For the more concrete form (4,2), namely $c(t, t-\tau) = x(t) \cdot a(t-\tau)$ this means that the function $a(t-\tau)$ is constant during the whole economic life of the project. Thus, the existing life of the investment project has no influence on the number of units produced $a(t-\tau)$. Costs arising at the project's old age are not expressed by the net cash flows as the component profit per unit $x(t)$ is only influenced by calendar time, i.e. it is mainly determined by the market price of the product.

Without loss of generality we assume in the following the function $x(t)$ to be scaled such that the constant number of produced units is equal to one, i.e. $a(t-\tau) \equiv 1$ (Marglin (1967), pp. 22).

For a given market interest rate m we start from the optimality condition (4,5) in order to determine the optimal construction date τ^*. We have $d[x(t)e^{-mt}]/\,dt = [x'(t) - mx(t)]e^{-mt}$. Assuming $\lim_{t\to\infty} x(t)e^{-mt} = 0$ we arrive at the simple first order condition for this special form of the model:

$$x(\tau^*) = mC\,. \tag{4,7}$$

In this case the optimal construction date τ^* of the project is the maximum point of the net present value function if the profit function $x(t)$ is strictly increasing, i.e. $x'(t) > 0$.

Now we compare the optimality conditions (4,5) and (4,7). If we neglect the age of the project, the optimal investment decision is quasi–myopic.

In (4,5) the marginal losses of the net cash flows of the whole project life are relevant to determine the optimal investment date. But optimality condition (4,7) only depends on the instantaneous profit. If the profit $x(\tau^*)$ at time τ^* equals the infinitesimal return on interest mC, the optimal decision is to undertake the investment project at τ^*, provided the profit function is strictly increasing.

We termed the optimal investment decision defined by optimality condition (4,7) quasi–myopic or equivalently quasi–static. This is in contrast to a myopic investment decision. An optimal decision is said to be myopic if the dynamics are completely ignored. According to (4,7) this situation would be obtained if the profit function is constant over the whole life of the project, namely $x(t) = mC$ for $t \geq \tau^*$. As easily can be checked, the myopic net present value is zero. In this way we arrive at the classical static NPV–rule, which has been discussed in the previous section in a discrete–time framework.

But the optimal construction date τ^* resulting from (4,7) only pretends myopic behaviour because of the special form of the optimality condition.

If we plug $C = x(\tau^*)/m$ in the NPV–function (4,4) for $a(t - \tau^*) \equiv 1$, we immediately obtain

$$(4,8) \qquad K^* := K(\tau^*, m) = \int_{\tau^*}^{\infty} x'(t)e^{-mt}/m\,dt > 0\,,$$

as we have $x'(t) > 0$ from the second order condition.

Contrary to the static NPV–rule, in this case the commitment at the optimal date τ^* results in a positive NPV. As soon as the discounted NPV K exceeds this positive NPV–premium, the investment project must be undertaken. On that account we term this optimal investment date τ^* quasi–myopic.

4.2.2 Optimal Timing of Investment and Interest Rate

Until now the interest rate m of a planning period has been assumed to be constant. In this section we investigate the effects of varying m with respect to the optimal investment date τ^* and the optimal net present value K^*.

There are two reasons for doing so. On the one hand, a comparison with the static net present value rule is established, and on the other hand, we also want to compare the deterministic dynamic model with the investment models under conditions of risk and uncertainty, respectively, which are studied in detail in the following sections.

As has to be expected, the general model characterized by assumptions C1 to C6 leads to no clear results (cp. Marglin (1967), pp. 32). Thus, we only consider the investment model whose net cash flows are independent of the project age.

Therefore, we state the corresponding first order condition (4,7) in dependence of the interest rate m:

$$x(\tau^*(m)) = mC\,.$$

Differentiating with respect to m yields

$$d\tau^*/dm = C/x'(t) > 0\,.$$

The r.h.s. of this expression is positive because of the second order condition $x'(t) > 0$.

Defining $K^*(m) := K(\tau^*(m), m)$, we obtain for the optimal NPV given by (4,8) as a function of the interest rate m:

$$dK^*/dm < 0 .$$

In this case a higher interest rate of a planning period, on the one hand, leads to the postponement of the optimal investment date τ^* but, on the other hand, causes a decrease of the optimal NPV K^*. The latter result is in accordance with the corresponding behaviour of the static NPV–function, provided the stream of net cash flows is simple (cp. section 4.1).

The following conclusion for this deterministic dynamic investment model with net cash flows independent of the project age can be drawn: The higher the interest rate m of a planning period, the lower are the discounted net cash flows and therefore also the lower is the positive NPV–premium K^*. Of course, this means that it is optimal to wait with investing in the project.

4.3 Investment Models Under Conditions of Risk

In the previous section we discussed a deterministic dynamic model to determine the optimal timing of investment for an indivisible and irreversible project. Now we remove one of the essential assumptions of this model, namely that the stream of net cash flows has to be known for certain at the beginning of the planning process. However, we do not consider these net cash flows themselves as random variables, but we concentrate on the (random) net present value and market value of the project, respectively. In this section we assume that the probability distribution of the market value is known to the investor in each planning period.

As we have already briefly mentioned in the introduction of this chapter, we analyze a real investment project which is traded on a perfect capital market. Thus, maximizing the project's market value under conditions of risk is also a justifiable goal from a theoretical point of view. Though this is only true if we impose an additional assumption.

If the real investment is not traded itself on the capital market, that is no market value can be observed, this market value must be replicable as linear combination of traded real and financial assets. In literature this property is called "spanning" (cp. e.g. Wilhelm (1983), pp. 527, Majd/Pindyck (1987), p. 10). In this case the distribution of the project's market value is given as the distribution of the sum of random variables of these independent assets. Their probability distributions are assumed to be known.

In literature many of the models dealing with the timing of investment under conditions of risk are not explicitly based on the valuation on the capital market. Therefore, we design in the following a simple model in this vein which in the subsequent section can be easily extended to a model for the timing of investment under conditions of uncertainty. We begin with the statement of the assumptions of the model which is again designed in a discrete–time framework. Afterwards we investigate the optimal investment strategy. Referring to our model we then briefly discuss models known from literature in discrete as well as in continuous time. Finally we perform several sensitivity investigations and develop an algorithm for computing the optimal investment policy. Some numerical results are presented.

4.3.1 Assumptions and the Optimal Investment Policy

In the following we put together the partly already known assumptions of the model:

D1. There are no taxes and transaction costs. The real investment project is independent of the other projects of the firm's investment program. Furthermore, the project is indivisible.

D2. The planning horizon T of the decision model is not larger than the economic life of the project.

In this way the irreversibility of the project within the planning horizon is well guaranteed. If T is equal to the economic life time, it is possible to analyze the impact of the project life on the optimal investment date.

D3. The model is designed in a discrete–time framework.

D4. The random market value of the project r_t can be observed at the beginning of each planning period $t = 1, \dots T+1$. It is described by the known and stationary probability distribution q.
The market values $r_1, \dots, r_{T+1}$ are stochastically independent over time.

The last assumption is just made for ease of presentation. Specifying the market values e.g. as Markov process or in dependence of a general state of the world causes no theoretical difficulties but only means an extension of the state space of the model.

D5. The opportunity M_t to undertake the project in planning period $t, 1 \leq t \leq T+1$, is a Bernoulli random variable with parameter p,

$0 < p \leq 1$. This means that the probability of an investment opportunity in a planning period is p. $M_1 \ldots, M_{T+1}$ are also stochastically independent (cp. e.g. Baldwin/Meyer (1979), Prastacos (1983)).

By an investment opportunity M_t in planning period t often the occurrence of a new kind of real investment is understood, e.g. in the sense of technical progress. But this interpretation is not suitable for our purposes as we assume the investment project to be fixed over the whole planning horizon.

Thus, it is not appropriate to base the valuation of an investment opportunity on the captial market. Instead we explain the occurrence of an opportunity to invest in a demand–oriented way. At the beginning of each planning period the future demand for the good is estimated which is produced by the investment project, e.g. a machine tool. If the expected demand exceeds a certain level d^*, the Bernoulli variable is set equal to one — in this case it pays to look whether it is optimal to undertake the project. But if in planning period t the expected future demand is lower than d^*, M_t is equal to zero — then in period t it is not invested at all.

As the project itself is valued on the capital market by observing its market value r_t in each planning period t, but the opportunity for investment characterized by the Bernoulli variable M_t is valued on the demand market, the following assumption is not too restrictive:

D6. The market values r_t and the investment opportunities M_t, $1 \leq t \leq T+1$, are stochastically independent.

As a consequence there is no difference between the marekt value if there exists an opportunity to invest and the market value in case of no investment opportunity.

D7. The initial capital cost of the project C is constant over the whole planning horizon. Before undertaking the project the amount C is not invested at the riskless rate of interest m.

D8. The aim of the investor is to maximize the discounted excess of the market value r over the initial capital cost C. The expected market value of the project is not smaller than the capital cost, i.e.

$$E(r) := \int r\, q(dr) \geq C\,.$$

D9. At the planning horizon T, i.e. at the beginning of planning period $T+1$, we distinguish two different ways of investment behaviour depending on contractual conditions:
  (I) There is no opportunity to invest.
  (II) If there exists an investment opportunity, i.e. $M_{T+1} = 1$, the project <u>must</u> be undertaken.

In case (I) the investor knows that in planning period T there is the last possibility for commitment. Contrary, in case (II) the investor can be faced with the situation to have to undertake the project although the market value r is smaller than the capital cost C. In terms of the deterministic static NPV–rule this means that the investment is not advantageous.

The last two assumptions indicate risk–neutral behaviour of the investor with respect to the goal–function. As maximization of the market value is the correct goal in investment analysis under conditions of risk, the assessment of utility is not suitable. But attitudes of risk and risk aversion can be expressed by means of the distribution q of the market values.

Another way to incorporate the firm–specific attitudes of risk and risk aversion is via the so–called risk–adjusted discount rate, or in our notion risk–adjusted interest rate. If the net cash flows of a project are risky, the appropriate interest rate for discounting the forecasted values is not the riskless rate m but the risk–adjusted interest rate which is greater than m, because risky projects are less desirable than safe ones (cp. e.g. Haley/Schall (1979), pp. 191 and pp. 316, Brealey/Myers (1981), chapter 9, Copeland/ Weston (1983), chapter 11).

In order to determine the discount factor β, we use the following rule of thumb for determining the risk–adjusted interest rate or the cost of capital of the project m_p:

D10. The opportunity cost of capital of the project m_p is given as follows:

(4,9) $$m_p = \lambda m_c + (1-\lambda)m\,.$$

The company cost of capital m_c is equal to the required return of the firm's securities. The rate of time preference is expressed by the riskless borrowing and lending rate m. Of course, m_c is not smaller than m. Parameter λ is a measure of the project's risk and also a measure of risk aversion of the investor. As usual the discount factor is defined by $\beta := 1/(1+m_p)$.

If $\lambda = 0$, we have $m_p = m$ indicating risk–neutral behaviour of the investor. Risk–averse attitudes are expressed by positive values of the "risk parameter" λ, because in this case the project cost of capital m_p is larger than the riskless interest rate m.

If $\lambda = 1$, we have $m_p = m_c$ meaning that the investment project has the same market risk as the firm's existing assets. Therefore, a project which is less risky than the existing business of the firm is characterized by a risk parameter λ between zero and one. If λ is greater than one, the investment project is more risky than the firm's current business.

There is, however, another well–known interpretation of equation (4,9) which describes the opportunity cost of capital of the project m_p. For this we rewrite (4,9) in the following manner:

$$m_p - m = \lambda(m_c - m)\,.$$

The risk–adjusted required expected rate of return for the project m_p can be determined by the Capital Asset Pricing Model (CAPM). In this case m_c denotes the expected rate of return on the market and λ defines the systematic risk of the project. In the CAPM–framework this risk parameter λ is usually called "beta". It expresses the sensitivity of the project's market value to movements in the capital market. The difference $m_p - m$ is termed the expected risk premium on the investment project whereas $m_c - m$ is the expected risk premium on the market.

But the CAPM is only valid if a number of assumptions is made. One assumption says that the rates of return of all risky assets are normally distributed (cp. e.g. Brealey/Myers (1981), chapter 8, Copeland/Weston (1983), p. 186).

Another difficulty arises when using the CAPM to determine the required rate of return of the project m_p. The standard CAPM is a single period model. Thus, is it justified to use the constant rate m_p for discounting in each planning period within the planning horizon ? The answer is yes if the project's future beta — in our case risk parameter λ — will be constant (cp. for these matters Copeland/Weston (1983), chapter 11).

But the use of a constant project cost of capital m_p means that the discount rate becomes lower as time evolves. In this way risk increases by a constant rate period by period. This corresponds with the opinion that distant cash flows or market values should be discounted at a higher rate than earlier ones.

As the specific assumptions of the CAPM are too narrowing for our model, we use the general equation (4,9) for computing the cost of capital of the project m_p instead. We conclude this discussion concerning the determination of the "correct" m_p by presenting a fundamental principle which does not depend on the CAPM: "Each project should be evaluated at its own opportunity cost of capital: the true cost of capital depends on the use to which the capital is put" (Brealey/Myers (1981), p. 183).

These ten assumptions are now used to formulate the corresponding dynamic program. From assumption D1 we know that the investment project is indivisible. Therefore the decision process may be stopped before the planning horizon T if the project is invested in one of the planning periods. Consequently we have to deal with a dynamic stopping decision model. In the dynamic programming formulation this fact is considered by introducing a decision–dependent discount factor.

These remarks lead to the 10–tupel $(Z, K, D, E, \overline{p}, q, w, \beta, g, \mathcal{J}_{T+1})$ of the following meaning:

a) the state space $Z := \{0,1\} \times \mathbf{R}$ with generic element $z = (i, r) \in Z$. If $i = 1(0)$ there is an (no) opportunity to invest in a planning period. $r \in \mathbf{R}$ represents the market value of the project at the beginning of a planning period.
b) the control space $K := \{0,1\}$. The investment project is (not) undertaken in the running planning period if $a = 1(0)$.
c) the set of admissible controls $D : Z \to \mathcal{P}(K)$, where $\mathcal{P}$ is the symbol for the power set. We have:

$$D(0, r) = \{0\} \quad , \quad D(1, r) = K\,.$$

Only in case there exists an opportunity to invest in a planning period the decision maker can choose between the two alternatives, namely to undertake the project or to wait with investment at least for one more period.
d) the disturbance space $E := \{0,1\} \times \mathbf{R}$ with $e := (j, \rho) \in E$. $j \in \{0,1\}$ says whether an investment opportunity exists in the subsequent planning period. The market value of the following period is denoted by $\rho \in \mathbf{R}$.
e) the disturbance distributions $\overline{p}$ and q. $\overline{p}$ is a probability distribution with values 0 and 1; $\overline{p}(\{1\}) = p$ is the probability for an investment opportunity in a planning period. The distribution of the market values is given by the probability distribution q with support $\mathbf{R}$.

f) the state transition function $w : Z \times K \times E \to Z$ is given by $w(z,a,e) = e$.

g) the discount factor $\beta : K \to [0,1]$. We have:

$$\beta(0) = \beta \in (0,1]\,, \quad \beta(1) = 0\,.$$

The latter specification guarantees that once the investment project is undertaken, the decision process is stopped.

h) the one–stage reward function $g : Z \times K \to \mathbf{R}$. We have:

$$g(i,r,0) \equiv 0\,, \quad g(1,r,1) = r - C\,.$$

i) the terminal reward function $\mathcal{J}_{T+1} : Z \to \mathbf{R}$. According to assumption D9 we have to consider two different specifications:

(4,10) $$\text{(I)} \quad \mathcal{J}_{T+1}(z) \equiv 0\,,$$

(4,11) $$\text{(II)} \quad \mathcal{J}_{T+1}(0,r) \equiv 0\,, \mathcal{J}_{T+1}(1,r) = r - C\,.$$

Contrary to chapter three in the following we do not specify the probability distribution q of the market value in detail. In order to ensure the reward functions to be bounded above, it is reasonable to assume the existence of a finite supremum $\bar{r} < \infty$ for the market value. In addition it is assumed that $E(r)$ exists, which is true for the distributions of chapter two.

Again we denote by $\mathcal{J}_t(z)$, $1 \leq t \leq T+1$, the maximal expected discounted reward from planning period t to the planning horizon $T+1$, starting at the beginning of t with state z. Due to the previously stated assumptions, these functions are well defined. They are computed by means of the value iteration procedure of dynamic programming.

For $t = T+1$ the value functions are given by (4,10) and (4,11), respectively. For $1 \leq t \leq T$ we have:

(4,12) $$\mathcal{J}_t(0,r) = \beta \int q(d\rho)[p\mathcal{J}_{t+1}(1,\rho) + (1-p)\mathcal{J}_{t+1}(0,\rho)]\,,$$

(4,13) $$\mathcal{J}_t(1,r) = \text{Max}\,\{r - C, \mathcal{J}_t(0,r)\}\,.$$

Thus, for $1 \leq t \leq T$ and $(i,r) \in Z$ the optimal investment policy is a finite sequence $(f_1, \ldots, f_T)$ of functions $f_t : Z \to K$, where

$$f_t(0,r) \equiv 0,$$

$$(4,14) \qquad f_t(1,r) = \begin{cases} 0 & \text{if } \; r - C \leq \mathcal{J}_t(0,r) \\ 1 & \text{otherwise}. \end{cases}$$

For $1 \leq t \leq T$ and $(i,r) \in Z$ we now define

$$(4,15) \qquad r_t^* := \operatorname{Inf}\{r \in \mathbf{R} \mid \mathcal{J}_t(0,r) \leq r - C\} \in [-\infty, \infty],$$

where $\operatorname{Inf}\phi := \infty$ and $\operatorname{Inf} \mathbf{R} := -\infty$.

The numbers r_t^* are called investment limits or option values. We show that the optimal investment decision functions $r \to f_t(1,r)$ given by (4,14) are nondecreasing. This means that the optimal investment policy is of control–limit type.

LEMMA 4.1. *For $1 \leq t \leq T$ and $(i,r) \in Z$ we have for the optimal investment decisions* (4,14):

$$f_t(1,r) = \begin{cases} 0 & \textit{if } \; r \leq r_t^* \\ 1 & \textit{otherwise}. \end{cases}$$

PROOF. *As $r \to \mathcal{J}_t(0,r)$ is constant, $r \to f_t(1,r)$ is nondecreasing.*

We assume that in planning period t an opportunity to undertake the real investment project, i.e. $i = 1$, exists. Then the commitment takes place if at the beginning of t the market value r of the project exceeds the investment limit r_t^*, otherwise the investor postpones the projcet for at least one period.

In this way the investor is sure that the excess of the market value over the capital cost $r - C$ is nonnegative in any case, as $\mathcal{J}_t(0,r) \geq 0, 1 \leq t \leq T$. This statement is always true for terminal reward specificaion (I) if the project cannot be undertaken at the planning horizon $T+1$. If at the planning horizon $T+1$ there is an opportunity to invest and the project must be undertaken (specification II), $\mathcal{J}_t(0,r) \geq 0$ is only valid because $E(r) \geq C$ by assumption D8.

In general the constant value function $\mathcal{J}_t(0,r)$ is positive. Further on we call it the NPV–premium. As the considered real investment project is an irreversible one, this NPV–premium has to be earned by the investor in order to compensate possible opportunity losses. Once the investor decides to undertake the project future investment opportunities with possibly higher excess market values are forfeited.

4.3.2 A Survey of Already Known Models

Now we compare the previously developed model for the determination of a project's optimal investment date under conditions of risk with related models already known from literature. We look at these models according to the following main characteristics:

1) discrete time — continuous time,
2) the market parameter used as state of the model,
3) the decision criterion, and
4) the admissible investment decisions.

The last characteristic mainly concentrates on the fact whether the investment project is divisible or indivisible. In case the project is divisible, the model is usually termed a sequential investment model.

We start with the discussion of models developed in a discrete–time framework. The model of Prastacos (1983) is very closely related to our model. The market parameter in his model is the quality of the investment project which is described by a nonnegative random variable. The occurrence of an investment opportunity in a planning period is characterized by the (constant) probability parameter p. In distinction from our model the investment project is assumed to be at any extent divisible. The capital cost of the project in all periods is C. As borrowing is not allowed, at most C monetary units can be spent for investing (there is no discounting). The amount of investment of a planning period is not limited.

Let I denote the amount invested in a planning period and let x be the quality of the project at the beginning of this period. Then this sequential investment policy is called optimal which maximizes the cumulative nondecreasing returns per period $R(I,x)$.

If the return function R is convex with respect to quality x, the optimal investment policy is of control–limit type. If in planning period t the quality x of the investment opportunity is not smaller than the "critical quality" x_t^*, the whole project is undertaken at once, i.e. the whole capital cost C is invested.

Contrary, if the return function R is concave in x, then in general it is optimal to split the investment project. Depending on the quality x of the opportunity in planning period t the amount I_t^* which must not be larger than the remaining capital is invested.

In section 4.3.1 we showed on the basis of an irreversible project the optimality of a control–limit policy for the linear "return function" r. This result coincides with that of Prastacos in case of a convex return function. Is is not surprising that in this situation the optimal investment policy for a divisible project is the same as that for an indivisible one. Of course, for a concave return function this correspondence is no longer valid.

Prastacos then determines explicitly the optimal investment policy for some specific return functions, as for example the linear, the power, and the logarithmic. The final part of the paper is devoted to the sensitivity analyses with respect to numerous parameters of the model.

Another model designed in a discrete–time framework is the one of Baldwin (1982). Here the market parameter is specified as the discrete state variable Q which describes the capacity or the output of the industry considered. The firm is assumed to operate in an imperfectly competitive industry, i.e. it exercises control over the state variable Q of the industry. Thus, the optimal investment policy differs from the standard NPV–rule.

Due to the exercised control over the industry the maintenance of the state Q is costly. Investments mean, on the one hand, expansion of capacity and higher output but, on the other hand, often decreasing prices. In this context Baldwin denotes an investment project irreversible if regaining the initial state of the industry, i.e the state with the old prices, can only be accomplished by some (transaction) costs (Baldwin (1982), p. 764).

The investment projects considered are not divisible. Again the goal of the firm is the maximization of the market value $R(Q)$ of the investment program. The state variable of the industry evolves according to a Markov chain. If in a planning period the existing investment opportunity is not taken, state Q remains unchanged during this period. Without explicitly assuming the monotonicity of the market value function $R(Q)$ here also the optimality of a control–limit policy is demonstrated.

In the second part of the work the model is applied to a firm which is engaged with the exploration and development of mines of non–renewable resources.

Moene (1985) discusses the optimal timing of a single irreversible project over an infinite planning horizon. Like in our model the investment project is assumed to be a durable productive asset. The optimal investment decision is not based on the market value of the project but depends on the output price, the wage rate, the capacity utilization, and on the initial capital cost. All these quantities are assumed to be random variables which are independent over time. Therefore, all markets are considered to be stationary. Contrary to the other discrete–time models, here the capital cost of the project is the state variable; it is independent of the other random quantities.

The optimal construction date is computed in accordance with the NPV of the project which in the paper is called the quasi rent. Hence, the investor is assumed to be risk–neutral. The optimal investment policy is of control–limit–type; it possesses the same features as that in our model: even when the investor observes a capital cost which yields an NPV between zero and the investment limit, he will not undertake the project. There is, however, a fundamental difference to the optimal investment policy of our model. In Moene's model the optimal decision rule is myopic due to the infinite planning horizon (Moene (1985), pp. 354).

The propensity to invest is defined by the probability to undertake the project in a planning period if the investor behaves optimally. It is shown how the propensity to invest depends on the probability distributions of the random variables and how it depends on the interest rate (Moene (1985), pp. 355).

Baldwin/Meyer (1979) investigate a model in a continuous time framework. They are dealing with the investment in a project over a finite or an infinite planning horizon which is at least irreversible in the short run and which is indivisible. Baldwin and Meyer are not interested in a single investment decision but in a sequence of such decisions where investment takes place in projects which are technically improved over time.

The opportunity to invest is not possible at any point in time but is dependent on the occurrence of a new production technology. The interarrival– time between two such opportunities is assumed to follow an exponential distribution with known and constant parameter. Thus, the dates possible for investment obey a Poisson process.

At such a point in time the investor can accept the opportunity or can leave it unused. If the project is undertaken, its economic life is also exponentially distributed with known and constant parameter.

The criterion for accepting or rejecting an investment opportunity as described earlier is in case of a finite planning horizon the cumulative output and in case of an infinite planning horizon the average output of the projects. In this framework implicitly risk neutrality, i.e. a linear utility function of the output, is assumed.

For subsequent investment opportunities the output of the project is characterized by independent random variables with stationary distribution. If an opportunity occurs, the output of the project is known to the investor. Thus, he must be in the position at this point in time to judge the PV of the project exactly.

Furthermore, the random processes — investment opportunity, economic life and output — are assumed to be stochastically independent of each other. In this context the independence of the output and the investment opportunity seems to be somewhat problematic. The stationarity of the distributions of the output hardly can be justified if the occurrence of an investment opportunity is identified with the existence of a new production technology.

Within the class of control–limit policies the optimal investment limit (hurdle rate) is determined in terms of the output of the project. Again the optimality of a control–limit policy is just stated and not proved as in our model.

We will later on return to the sensitivity investigations that are performed in the final section of Baldwin/Meyer (1979).

In the following we review continuous–time models for the determination of the optimal investment date of an irreversible project which are explicitly based on valuation on the capital markets. The model's market parameter is usually described by specific continuous–time Markov processes. These so–called diffusion processes are commonly given in the form of a stochastic differential equation. Because the detailed presentation of this theory would be by far beyond the scope of this work, we will limit ourselves to an informal overview (for the applications of stochastic processes in this framework we refer to Malliaris/Brock (1982)).

But we demonstrate the basic concepts of one stream of these models. The analysis is kept as simple as possible to stress the essence of the problem and to obtain a closed–form solution (cp. Heaney/Jones (1988), pp. 3).

Over an infinite planning horizon a risk–neutral investor has to decide when to invest in an indivisible project. At time $t = 0$, the beginning of the decision process, the NPV of the project $K(0) = K_0$ is known. Future NPVs are represented by the following stochastic process, given by the corresponding stochastic differential equation:

$$dK(t) = \sigma\, dz(t)\,.$$

$K(t)$ denotes the NPV at time t, $z(t)$ is the standard Wiener process, σ^2 is the constant instantaneous variance of the NPV, and finally d denotes the differential operator. The drift of this stochastic differential equation is equal to zero. This means that the expected NPV of the project K_0 is constant over time. Thus, the project's NPV $K(t)$ fluctuates around the expected NPV over time. The amplitude of these fluctuations is determined by the variance σ^2.

We restrict the analysis to the computation of the optimal investment date within the class of stationary control–limit policies. If $\overline{K}$ denotes the critical NPV, the project immediately is undertaken at $t = 0$ provided $K_0 \geq \overline{K}$. Contrary, suppose $K_0 < \overline{K}$ holds. Then investment takes place when for the first time $K(t) \geq \overline{K}$, $t > 0$, is satisfied.

$\overline{K}$ is determined such that the expected NPV discounted to time $t = 0$ is maximized. For that purpose we need the distribution of the first passage time τ from K_0 to $\overline{K}$, provided K_0 is less than $\overline{K}$. Its density is denoted by $\pi(\tau|K_0, \overline{K})$ and is of the following form (cp. e.g. Fahrmeir et al. (1981), pp. 188):

$$\pi(\tau|K_0, \overline{K}) = (\overline{K} - K_0)(2\pi\sigma^2\tau^3)^{-\frac{1}{2}} \exp[-(\overline{K} - K_0)^2/(2\sigma^2\tau)]\,.$$

Thus, the goal function is given by:

$$\begin{aligned}\kappa(\overline{K}) &= \overline{K} \int_0^\infty e^{-m\tau} \pi(\tau|K_0, \overline{K})\, d\tau \\ &= \overline{K} \exp[(K_0 - \overline{K})(2m)^{\frac{1}{2}}/\sigma]\,.\end{aligned}$$

Consequently, the optimal critical NPV is

$$\overline{K} = \sigma/(2m)^{\frac{1}{2}}\,. \tag{4,16}$$

Equation (4,16) expresses two important properties of the optimal investment behaviour. On the one hand, high risk represented by a high value of σ leads to a high critical NPV $\overline{K}$. Therefore, it is more likely that the project will be postponed. On the other hand, this behaviour is also obtained by a decrease of the (riskfree) interest rate m. We will return to these properties during the discussion of the model under conditions of uncertainty.

A similar model is developed by Mc Donald/Siegel (1986). They also study the optimal timing of investment in an irreversible project over an infinite planning horizon. The market parameter is defined as the present value of the projects, which in many applications is the market value of an asset. The present value as well as the capital cost of the project follow geometric Wiener processes. Risk aversion is introduced by assuming that the investors hold well–diversified portfolios. In this way the opportunity cost of capital of the project m_p — see (4,9) — is derived as the equilibrium expected rate of return on the investment opportunity. Under these assumptions the solution of the investment model can be computed in explicit form by using techniques of the theory of stochastic differential equations. It is optimal to undertake the project if the ratio of present value and capital cost exceeds a critical number. Thus, the optimal investment policy is stationary and of control–limit type.

But the previously sketched solution method becomes rather complicated if other stochastic processes and/or a finite planning horizon are assumed. Also the solution by means of stochastic control theory methods is associated with insurmountable difficulties.

Another approach in the continuous–time framework is the so–called option pricing theory. This theory enables the preference–free valuation of options to a large extent, i.e. the explicit knowledge of the return expectations as well as the utility assessment of the investor is not necessary.

This approach leads to a valuation equation where in our situation the value of the project is related to the underlying market parameter. Often the market parameter is specified as the project's market value which follows a diffusion process, e.g. a geometric Wiener process. In our discrete–time model from section 4.3.1 the above mentioned value of the project is given by the value function $\mathcal{J}_t(0,r)$ in (4,12).

In order to derive a valuation equation at any point in time in a perfect capital market, a hedge portfolio must exist. For example, a hedge portfolio consists of the market value and the (short–sold) value of the project with the expected rate of return of this portfolio being equal to the risk-free interest rate m. Thus, the hedge portfolio is composed such that no arbitrage profits can be realized. The best known option–valuation model is that by Black/Scholes (1973). There the value of a European call option written on a common stock which pays no dividends until the expiration date is determined. Contrary to an American call option, a European call option can only be exercised at one date, the expiration date.

This theory is used by Heaney and Jones in a somewhat generalized setting to determine the optimal investment date for an irreversible and indivisible project with constant capital cost (cp. Heaney/Jones (1988), pp. 5). The market parameter is originally defined as a general one–dimensional state of the world but is then specified as the market value of the (new) project. If this state follows a geometric Wiener process closed–form solutions of the critical market value (the investment limit) can be computed, provided the analysis is again limited to stationary control–limit policies.

Majd/Pindyck (1987) also use this approach but consider a divisible investment project. In this way the time to construct the project is included in form of a linear network. Contrary to Prastacos (1983), Majd and Pindyck assume a maximum rate at which investment and construction can proceed, i.e. it takes time to build the project. Obviously the state of the model becomes two–dimenional. In addition to the project's market value which again follows a geometric Wiener process the total amount already invested has to be taken into account. The whole capital cost of the project is known. Clearly the control variable is the rate of investment. For this model the optimal investment policy is a combined "bang–bang" and control– limit rule. If the market value exceeds the investment limit, it is optimal to invest at the maximum rate. If the market value is lower than this limit, the instantaneous level of investment is zero.

The optimal solution is determined by means of two valuation equations, one for the case investment takes place and the other for the no–investment situation. It may happen that it is optimal to construct only part of the project. In our opinion this may limit the practical meaning of the model. The optimal solution must be computed numerically.

All in all the theory of option pricing is a very promising approach for valuing real assets. This value of the asset (project) is then used to make the optimal investment decision. Often it is not clear whether a control–limit policy is in fact optimal. Explicit results in form of closed–form solutions are only obtained if the stochastic process governing the market parameter of the model is a geometric Wiener process. Consequently, most of the sensitivity results are also limited to this specific assumption.

We continue by presenting sensitivity investigations for our model developed in section 4.3.1 for a general distribution of the market value.

4.3.3 Sensitivity Analyses and an Algorithm

We perform sensitivity analyses with respect to parameters of our model from section 4.3.1. We concentrate on those parameters which also have been the subject of sensitivity investigations in the models previously reviewed. Then we present an algorithm for the computation of the optimal investment policy, i.e. the investment limits and NPV–premiums. We use this algorithm to compute some numerical results for Erlang–distributed market values.

Before starting we agree upon the following notational convention: We always select one parameter of the model and keep the others constant. We specify two distinct values of the parameter, e.g. p_1 and p_2 with $p_1 < p_2$, and compare the corresponding value functions $\mathcal{J}_t^j$, optimal investment decisions f_t^j and investment limits r_t^j, $j = 1, 2$.

First of all we investigate the influence on the optimal investment decisions if the probability p of an investment opportunity M_t is varied.

LEMMA 4.2. *(Variation of p) Let $p_1, p_2 \in (0,1]$ with $p_1 < p_2$. Then we have for $1 \leq t \leq T$ and $z = (i, r) \in Z$:*

a) $\mathcal{J}_t^1(z) \leq \mathcal{J}_t^2(z)$,
b) $f_t^1(1,r) \geq f_t^2(1,r)$ and $r_t^1 \leq r_t^2$.

PROOF. *We proceed by backward induction. We start with $t = T$. Obviously, if $i = 0$, a) is satisfied in case of the terminal reward function (4,10). For specification (4,11) a) follows for $i = 0$ because of assumption D8. As a) is also valid for $i = 1$, the same is true for b).*

Now we turn to the general induction step. Let a) and b) be satisfied for $t + 1 \leq \tau \leq T$. Then we have:

$$\begin{aligned}
\mathcal{J}_t^1(0,r) &= \beta \int q(d\rho)\{p_1[\mathcal{J}_{t+1}^1(1,\rho) - \mathcal{J}_{t+1}^1(0,\rho)] + \mathcal{J}_{t+1}^1(0,\rho)\} \\
&\leq \beta \int q(d\rho)\{p_2[\mathcal{J}_{t+1}^1(1,\rho) - \mathcal{J}_{t+1}^1(0,\rho)] + \mathcal{J}_{t+1}^1(0,\rho)\} \\
&\leq \mathcal{J}_t^2(0,r).
\end{aligned}$$

The first inequality holds because we always have $\mathcal{J}_t(1,r) \geq \mathcal{J}_t(0,r)$. *Thus, a) is also satisfied for* $i = 1$ *implying the validity of b).*

A high probability p_2 for an opportunity to invest in planning period t leads to a high NPV–premium $\mathcal{J}_t^2(0,r)$ and therefore to a high investment limit r_t^2. In such a situation the investor prefers to postpone the project.

This result is quite reasonable. If this probability p decreases the frequency of arriving investment opportunities also goes down. Therefore, the investor cannot be particular in his commitments. This is in accordance with the sensitivity result of Baldwin and Meyer for the parameter of the exponential distribution describing the interarrival time between two opportunities (Baldwin/Meyer (1979), p. 363).

Next we consider the effect on the investment decisions if the planning horizon T is varied.

LEMMA 4.3. *(Variation of* T*) Let* T_1 *and* T_2 *with* $T_1 < T_2$ *be given. Then we have for* $1 \leq t \leq T$ *and* $z = (i,r) \in Z$*:*

a) $\mathcal{J}_t^1(z) \leq \mathcal{J}_t^2(z)$,
b) $f_t^1(1,r) \geq f_t^2(1,r)$ and $r_t^1 \leq r_t^2$.

PROOF. *It is enough to show the assertion for* $T_1 := T$ *and* $T_2 := T+1$. *We start with considering planning period* $T+1$. *For the terminal reward function (4,10) we have:*

$$\mathcal{J}_{T+1}^1(0,r) = \mathcal{J}_{T+1}^2(0,r) \equiv 0\,,$$
$$\mathcal{J}_{T+1}^1(1,r) \equiv 0 \leq Max\{r - C, 0\} = \mathcal{J}_{T+1}^2(1,r)\,.$$

For the terminal reward function (4,11) we obtain:

$$\mathcal{J}_{T+1}^1(0,r) \equiv 0\,, \quad \mathcal{J}_{T+1}^1(1,r) = r - C\,,$$
$$\mathcal{J}_{T+1}^2(0,r) = \beta p \int q(d\rho)[\rho - C]\,,$$
$$\mathcal{J}_{T+1}^2(1,r) = Max\{r - C\,, \mathcal{J}_{T+1}^2(0,r)\}\,.$$

Remember that $E(r) \geq C$ *by assumption D8. Hence we have:*

$$\mathcal{J}_{T+1}^1(z) \leq \mathcal{J}_{T+1}^2(z)\,.$$

Now assertions a) and b) can be proved by the procedure of backward induction in the usual way.

Thus, the larger the planning horizon of the investor is, the more likely he will postpone the project which is expressed by a higher NPV–premium and a higher investment limit. Now suppose the investor must undertake the project at the planning horizon if there exists an opportunity to invest (terminal reward specification II, see assumption D9). Then the conclusion of the previous lemma is only valid because the expected market value of the project must not be smaller than its capital cost (see assumption D8).

As the real investment project under consideration is irreversible in fact, we have assumed that its planning horizon must not exceed its economic life (see assumption D2). If a positive relationship between project life and planning horizon exists, an increase in the planning horizon means that the project life goes up. Consequently the investor must "live" with his project for a longer time. But then it is clear that he can use this "extra" time to wait for a really good investment opportunity. This is indeed the message of the previous lemma; it is in correspondence with the result of Baldwin and Meyer (cp. Baldwin/Meyer (1979), p. 363).

Finally, we investigate the sensitivity with respect to the probability distribution of the market value q.

Therefore, we compare probability distributions in two different ways. The first comparison is carried out by first order stochastic dominance. Probability distribution q_2 dominates q_1 with respect to first order stochastic dominance,abbreviated by $q_1 <_1 q_2$, if $q_1(B) \leq q_2(B)$ for all increasing sets $B \subseteq \mathbf{R}$ (see the remarks following Theorem 3.1).

The second comparison is made by a relation which is complementary to second order stochastic dominance defined by Theorem 3.1, provided the two distributions have the same expected value.

Suppose that q_1 and q_2 have the same expected value. Then we say that q_2 dominates q_1 in the sense of relation $<_v$, i.e. $q_1 <_v q_2$, if

$$\int h(r) q_1(dr) \leq \int h(r) q_2(dr)$$

for all convex functions $h : \mathbf{R} \to \mathbf{R}$ whose integrals with respect to q_1 and q_2 exist. This is Stoyan's relation $\leq_c$ (cp. Stoyan (1983), pp. 8).

If $q_1 <_v q_2$ then q_1 dominates q_2 in the sense of second order stochastic dominance (cp. Stoyan (1983), p. 12).

Now we are in the position to state the sensitivity result:

LEMMA 4.4. *(Variation of q) Let two probability distributions q_1 and q_2 be given. Assume $q_1 <_1 q_2$ or $q_1 <_v q_2$.*
Then we have for $1 \leq t \leq T+1$ and $z = (i,r) \in Z$:

a) $\mathcal{J}_t^1(z) \leq \mathcal{J}_t^2(z)$,
b) $f_t^1(1,r) \geq f_t^2(1,r)$ and $r_t^1 \leq r_t^2$.

PROOF. *We only prove the assertions of the lemma for the stochastic dominance relation "$<_v$". According to its definition the value functions $\mathcal{J}_t^j(i,r)$, $j = 1,2$ must be convex with respect to r.*

Now $\mathcal{J}_t^j(0,r)$ is a constant, and $\mathcal{J}_t^j(1,r) = \mathrm{Max}\{r - C, \mathcal{J}_t^j(0,r)\}$. Therefore $r \to \mathcal{J}_t^j(1,r)$ is also convex.

In order to interpret these results we use the following notational convention: $E_j(r^k) := \int r^k q_j(dr)$, $k \geq 0$; the variance of distribution q_j is denoted by $\mathrm{Var}_j(r)$, $j = 1,2$.

If the market value distributions q_1 and q_2 are ordered in the sense of first order stochastic dominance, i.e. $q_1 <_1 q_2$, we always have $E_1(r^k) \leq E_2(r^k)$, provided the market value is a nonnegative random variable.

Especially this means that $q_1 <_1 q_2$ implies $E_1(r) < E_2(r)$. Thus, the higher the expected value of the market value, the higher is the corresponding NPV–premium and the higher is also the investment limit. In such a situation the investor thinks to realize a relatively high market value when undertaking the project, and therefore his respective expectations are also quite high.

Now assume that the market value distributions q_1 and q_2 are ordered by $q_1 <_v q_2$. If the market value is a nonnegative random variable, we have $E_1(r^k) \leq E_2(r^k)$ for $k > 1$. As in this case $E_1(r) = E_2(r)$ we always obtain $\mathrm{Var}_1(r) \leq \mathrm{Var}_2(r)$. This resulting ordering of the variances also explains the subscript "v" in the symbol "$<_v$".

If the market value distribution q_2 is more risky than q_1 — risk is in this way exclusively defined by means of the variance —, then investment limit r_t^2 is not smaller than r_t^1. When we start from equal expected market values a higher variance leads to a more cautious behaviour of the investor.

Especially this latter fact can be found in almost all papers reviewed in the previous section. This holds for the discrete–time model of Prastacos (1983), for the continuous–time model of Baldwin/Meyer (1979) as well as for the "diffusion"–models of Mc Donald/Siegel (1986) and Majd/Pindyck

(1987). Only in the model of Heaney and Jones an increase in the instantaneous variance of the market value may lead to a decrease of the investment limit. But this effect depends on the growth rate of the project and on the risk adjusted discount rate (cp. Heaney/Jones (1988), p. 12).

In the final part of this section we present an algorithm for computing the optimal investment limits r_t^*, $1 \leq t \leq T$. A similar algorithm has been developed by Prastacos for the case of a linear return function (cp. Prastacos (1983), Theorem 4.1).

We know that in each planning period the value functions if no investment opportunity arrives $\mathcal{J}_t(0,r)$, $1 \leq t \leq T+1$, are constant with respect to the market value r. Therefore, we agree upon the following abbreviation:

$$\mathcal{J}_t^* := \mathcal{J}_t(0,r)\,, \quad 1 \leq t \leq T+1\,.$$

The NPV–premiums $\mathcal{J}_t^*$ as well as the investment limits r_t^*, $1 \leq t \leq T$, can be computed recursively in the following way. This can be proved easily by backward induction.

1) Let $t = T$.
2) For terminal reward function (I) let $\mathcal{J}_t^* = 0$;
   for terminal reward function (II) let $\mathcal{J}_t^* = \beta p \int (r - C) q(dr)$.
3) Let $r_t^* = \mathcal{J}_t^* + C$.
4) Let $t = t - 1$.
5) If $t \leq 0$ then STOP.
6) Let $\mathcal{J}_t^* = \beta[(1-p)\mathcal{J}_{t+1}^* + p\mathcal{J}_{t+1}^* F(r_{t+1}^*) + p\int_{r_{t+1}^*}^{\infty} (r - C) q(dr)]$.
7) Goto 3).

In 6) F denotes the distribution function of the probability distribution q.

$\mathcal{J}_t^*$ and r_t^* can be computed analytically if closed–form expressions for the distribution function F and for the integral in 6) exist. Otherwise numerical methods must be employed.

In order to show that investment timing considerations are quantitatively important, we present some numerical results for reasonable parameter values.

We take the family of Erlang distributions as candidate for the distribution of the market value. An Erlang distribution is a special Gamma distribution $G(\alpha, \theta)$ with parameter α being an integer (see Table 2.1). Its expected value is $E(r) = \alpha/\theta$, the variance is $\mathrm{Var}(r) = \alpha/\theta^2$, and the skewness is $\gamma(r) = 2/\sqrt{\alpha}$. We take the Erlang distribution to avoid the use of numerical methods mentioned above. Furthermore, the positive skewness of this distribution allows the investor to express his degree of risk–averse behaviour.

We present the numerical results only for the terminal reward specification (I).

The reference model is defined by the following values of the parameters:

$$T = 5\,, \quad p = 0.8\,, \quad \alpha = \theta = 2\,, \quad C = 1\,, \quad m_c = 0.08\,, \quad m = 0.04\,, \quad \lambda = 1.5\,.$$

Therefore, $E(r) = 1$, i.e. the expected market value equals the initial capital cost C. The variance is $\mathrm{Var}(r) = 0.5$ and the skewness is $\gamma(r) = \sqrt{2}$.

The cost of capital of the project can be computed by (4,9) $m_p = 0.1$. The resulting discount factor is $\beta = 0.9091$.

The investment limits r_t^* for the reference model are as follows:

t	1	2	3	4	5
r_t^*	1.48	1.41	1.32	1.20	1.00

Thus, for reasonable parameter values it is optimal to undertake the project immediately, i.e. in planning period one, if the market value is almost 50% larger than the capital cost of the project.

If the probability for an investment opportunity is decreased to $p = 0.5$, the investment limit of the first planning period r_1^* goes down to 1.34.

Increasing the planning horizon from 5 to 10 periods increases r_1^* to 1.64.

Now we vary the parameters of the market value distribution. Two Erlang distributions q_1 and q_2 are ordered in the sense of first order stochastic dominance, i.e. $q_1 <_1 q_2$, if $\alpha_1 \leq \alpha_2$ and/or $\theta_1 \geq \theta_2$.

An increase of parameter α from 2 to 2.5 means an increase of the expected market value to 1.25 and of the variance to 0.625; only skewness decreases in this case. Here investment in the first planning period is optimal only if the market value of the project is nearly double the capital cost, namely $r_1^* = 1.90$.

Two Erlang distributions q_1 and q_2 are ordered by "$<_v$", i.e. $q_1 <_v q_2$, if $\alpha_1 \geq \alpha_2$. If we increase parameter α to 4, we also have to increase θ

to 4 because the expected market value has to remain constant $E(r) = 1$. The variance decreases in this case to 0.25; also the skewness goes down to 1.

As this project is less risky than the reference project, its first period investment limit r_1^* is only 1.34.

Finally, we vary two model parameters where no sensitivity analysis has been peformed. Clearly an increase of the initial capital cost C causes the postponement of the project. If the capital cost is 1.1 instead of 1, in the first planning period the investment limit goes up from 1.48 to 1.53.

As the risk parameter λ is greater than one, the reference project is more risky than the firm's current business. If we change the risk parameter to $\lambda = 0.5$, the resulting project is less risky than the existing business of the firm. In this case the cost of capital of the project m_p is 0.06 and the discount factor β is 0.9434.

As a consequence the first period's investment limit r_1^* increases to 1.52. Thus, the less risky the investor values the project, the more he expects from it. Remember that an increase of the risk parameter λ also means increasing risk–aversion of the investor. Therefore, high risk–aversion implies low investment limits and NPV–premiums, i.e. high risk–aversion is equivalent to an attitude towards investment.

We shall come back to the sensitivity analysis with respect to the risk parameter λ and with respect to the riskfree interest rate m in course of the next section when analyzing the investment model under conditions of uncertainty.

4.4 Investment Models under Conditions of Uncertainty

In the conclusions of their work Baldwin and Meyer identify five major restrictive assumptions (cp. Baldwin/Meyer (1979), pp. 368). These are the following:

1) the linear utility function,
2) the same probability for the occurrence of an investment opportunity in each planning period,
3) the fixed economic life of the project,
4) the stationary probability distribution of the market parameter, in their model the output of the project, and finally
5) the indivisibility of the irreversible investment project.

A look at section 4.3.1 shows that our model is also based on these five assumptions. Because we specify the market parameter as the market value of the project, the linear utility function is the correct goal function of the investor. Therefore, assumption 1) from above is in our case no essential restriction for the model. Whereas we continue to analyze an indivisible and irreversible investment project with fixed economic life and thus approximately known planning horizon of the model, we abandon assumptions 2) and 4) from above.

We consider again constant probabilities and stationary distributions, respectively, but now assume that at the beginning of the planning process they are unknown and depend on an unknown parameter, respectively. As a consequence, we determine in this section the optimal investment date of the project not under conditions of risk but under conditions of uncertainty.

In the following we formulate these conditions under uncertainty explicitly as new assumptions of our model. Afterwards we translate them to a binary stopping decision model. Then we compare the properties of the optimal investment policy with those of already known models. Finally we perform extensive sensitivity analyses, namely with respect to the capital cost, the interest rate, the planning horizon, and the prior distributions. Moreover, we compare the optimal policy with the certainty equivalence policy and we present special properties of the model without discounting. Most parts of this section are also contained in Benzing/Jammernegg (1988).

We start with an illustrative example which demonstrates the influence of uncertainty on the optimal investment decision, but for a reversible real asset.

4.4.1 The Influence of Uncertainty: An Example

We begin the discussion of investment under conditions of uncertainty by considering a reversible real investment project whose net present value (NPV) is a random variable. As the project is a reversible one, we can limit ourselves to a static analysis. For this kind of model we use the following generalized NPV–rule: Accept the investment project if the probability of negative NPV–realizations is not larger than a prespecified number ϵ, $0 < \epsilon < 1$. Denoting the NPV by K, the project is undertaken if

$$P(K < 0) \leq \epsilon .$$

Now suppose the project's NPV K follows a Normal distribution with initially unknown expected value θ but known variance $\sigma^2 = 16$, i.e. $K \sim N(\theta, 16)$. Furthermore, the investor is assumed to know the average NPV $\overline{K} = 10$ from $n = 10$ equivalent projects from the past. He has also the possibility of expressing his subjective beliefs with respect to this unknown parameter θ by an a priori distribution, say $\theta \sim N(10, 9)$.

In the following we distinguish between three types of investors: the first one only uses the (objective) sample data, the second investor just uses subjective data in form of the prior distribution whereas the third investor takes objective as well as subjective data into consideration.

a) The traditional investor bases his decision exclusively on sample data. As the sample mean $\overline{K}$ is an unbiased estimator for θ, this investor takes $\overline{K} = 10$ as point estimate. Thus, the distribution of the NPV becomes the $N(10, 16)$–distribution. As a consequence we have:

$$P(K < 0) = 0.0062 .$$

b) The Bayesian investor uses exclusively subjective information. This investor determines the posterior distribution for K by means of the prior distribution for θ without using sample data, i.e. he starts from the information state $(n, y) = (0, 0)$. From Table 2.2 the posterior distribution for K is given as the $N(10, 25)$–distribution. Thus we have:

$$P(K < 0) = 0.0228 .$$

c) The adaptive investor uses subjective as well as objective information. In this case the posterior distribution for the NPV K is not only determined by the prior distribution $N(10, 9)$ for the unknown parameter θ but also by the sample information state $(n, y) = (10, 100)$. According to Table 2.2 K is $N(10, 17.36)$–distributed. Consequently we obtain:

$$P(K < 0) = 0.0082 .$$

Now choose $\epsilon = 0.01$ as the critical probability for the occurrence of negative net present values out of the project. In this situation the traditional investor decides to undertake the project whereas the Bayesian one rejects it. But if the Bayesian investor converts to an adaptive investor by including the sample information in the investment decision, he accepts the project.

What is the explanation for such a different investment behaviour, although the expected value of the prior distribution coincides with the sample mean $\overline{K} = 10$ which in any case leads to the expected NPV of 10?

The traditional investor only takes the point estimate for θ into account but not the estimation error which here is expressed by the variance of K. The Bayesian investor is aware of this estimation risk, thereby increasing the variance of the NPV from 16 to 25. Thus, it is not surprising that the probability for rejecting the project almost quadruples, namely from 0.0062 to 0.0228. This also leads to a change of the investment decision. But from case c) we see that the sample size n of the objective data plays a key role in distinguishing between the traditional and the Bayesian approach. The sample size of $n = 10$ considerably decreases the variance of the NPV. The variance of the NPV of the adaptive investor is only slightly higher than the original variance, namely 17.36 to 16. This in turn means that the project is accepted. Of course, in reality an investor hardly will be in the position to have such extensive sample information, but he will have to be confident with much smaller sample sizes.

The following conclusions can be drawn from this simple example: In order to meet the optimal (or: correct) investment decisions under conditions of uncertainty, the estimation risk must be included in the decision process in an appropriate manner which here has been achieved by the Bayesian approach. More general analyses on this subject can be found in the work of Chen/Moore (1982).

We shall think over this just mentioned aspect in the following dynamic model for the determination of the optimal investment date of an indivisible, irreversible project.

4.4.2 The Explicit Formulation of Uncertainty

Contrary to the model under conditions of risk from section 4.3.1 we now suppose that at the beginning of the planning process the probability for an opportunity to invest in a period is unknown as is a parameter of the distribution of the project's market value. In both cases the investor is assumed to be in the position to condense the obtained "soft" market data, previously called subjective information, to an a priori distribution. Including the actual "hard" market data, here the market values, the posterior probability of an investment opportunity as well as the posterior distribution of the market value is then determined via the Bayesian theorem.

The basis on which the investment decisions are made is also slightly modified. Therefore, we start from the system of assumptions D1 - D10 of the model under conditions of risk. In the following we state only those assumptions which have been changed:

D4'. r_t, $-L \leq t \leq T+1$, denotes the random market value of the project in planning period t, where r_t is assumed to be observable at the beginning of period t. The market values $r_{-L}, \ldots, r_1$, $L \in \mathbf{N}_0 \cup \{-1\}$ represent the existing prior information of hard data at the beginning of the planning process, i.e. at the beginning of period one. The distribution ν_θ of the market value r_t depends on an unknown parameter $\theta \in \Theta \subseteq \mathbf{R}$. In the following we limit ourselves to the discussion of the continuous distributions ν_θ from Table 2.1, namely the Gamma, the Lognormal and the Normal distribution.

For given parameter $\theta \in \Theta$ the market values $r_{-L}, \ldots, r_{T+1}$ constitute an *iid* sequence of random variables.

At the beginning of each planning period t, $1 \leq t \leq T+1$, we know from chapter 2 for the specified distributions ν_θ the existence of a one–dimensional sufficient statistic $b = T(r_{-L}, \ldots, r_t)$. The information state at the beginning of period t is represented by (k, b) where $k := L + 1 + t$.

In a Bayesian manner the investor is able to specify for the unknown parameter θ a prior distribution $\overline{\mu}_r$ which summarizes the subjective information at the beginning of the planning process.

Starting from information state (k, b) at the beginning of planning period t the posterior distribution μ_r for θ is given by the transition probability $(tp)\mu_r(k, b; \cdot)$ as defined in (2,4):

$$\mu_r(k, b; D) = \int_D g(k, b; \theta)\overline{\mu}_r(d\theta) / \int_\Theta g(k, b; \theta')\overline{\mu}_r(d\theta'), \tag{4,17}$$

where $D \subseteq \Theta$.

$g(k, b; \theta)$ denotes the density function of the sufficient statistic $b = T(r_{-L}, \ldots, r_t)$ in dependence of the unknown parameter θ.

The posterior distribution of the market value r_{t+1} is specified by $tp\,q$ as defined in (2,5):

$$q(k,b;B) = \int_{\Theta} \nu_\theta(B)\mu_r(k,b;\,d\theta)\,, \quad k \in \mathbf{N}\,,\ b \in \mathbf{R}\,,\ B \subseteq \mathbf{R}\,. \tag{4,18}$$

D5'. In period t the investment opportunity M_t, $-L' \le t \le T+1$, is a Bernoulli random variable with unknown probability parameter π. The sample $M_{-L'},\ldots,M_1$, $L' \in \mathbf{N}_0 \cup \{-1\}$, characterizes the information available at the beginning of the planning process.

Given parameter π the random variables $M_{-L'},\ldots,M_{T+1}$ are stochastically independent and identically distributed.

We know from chapter 2 that $y = M_{-L'}+\cdots+M_t$, $1 \le t \le T+1$, is a one–dimensional sufficient statistic for $(M_{-L'},\ldots,M_t)$. For $n := L'+1+t$, (n,y) is the information state of the investor at the beginning of planning period t. There y denotes the number of periods from $-L'$ on with the opportunity to undertake the project.

At the beginning of the planning process the subjective information relevant for parameter π is summarized by the a priori distribution $\overline{\mu}_p$ on the unit interval whose support must not be concentrated on the set $\{0,1\}$.

If in planning period t the information state is (n,y), the posterior probability for an investment opportunity in this period is given by means of (2,4) and (2,5) by the Bayesian theorem as follows:

$$p(n,y) = \int_0^1 \pi^{y+1}(1-\pi)^{n-y}\overline{\mu}_p(d\pi) \Big/ \int_0^1 \pi^{y}(1-\pi)^{n-y}\overline{\mu}_p(d\pi)\,. \tag{4,19}$$

D8'. The investor makes his decision on the basis of

$$N(k,b) := \int q(k,b;\,dr)r - C\,, \tag{4,20}$$

where $N(k,b)$ is the posterior expected market value less the capital cost C of the project which are assumed to be constant over the whole planning horizon. We call $N(k,b)$ in the following the posterior expected "net present value".

Remember that in the model under conditions of risk the investment decision is made according to $r - C$ (see assumption D8). What is now the reason for departing from that and for using (4,20) as decision criterion instead ?

On the one hand, the use of $N(k, b)$ takes the possible occurrence of delivery times or ordering times into consideration. In this way also the time to build the project like the set up or installation of a machine can be incorporated in the decision rule. So the first cash flows from the investment project are obtained one period after the commitment. Especially Majd/Pindyck (1987) emphasize this important aspect of the consideration of the project's construction or set up period. Thus, it seems to be plausible to take instead of the actual market value r the conditional expected net present value $N(k, b)$ as decision criterion because in the latter case the whole information with respect to the market value is involved.

On the other hand, an investor using $r - C$ as decision rule is in a dilemma if the periodically observed market values fluctuate irregularly, i.e. if no explicit positive or negative trend in the market values can be recognized. What is the "true" distribution of the market value in such a situation? If the planning horizon of a model for the determination of the optimal investment date is not too long, it seems to be sensible to control such short–term fluctuations by a decision rule of the form (4,20), namely $N(k, b)$. In this way it is possible to smooth these irregularities.

At the planning horizon we distinguish again the two possibilities of the model under conditions of risk (see assumption D9), namely:

(I) There is no opportunity to invest.
(II) If there exists an opportunity, the project must be undertaken.

In case (II) the investor now obtains $N(k, b)$ instead of $r - C$.

4.4.3 The Description as Binary Stopping Decision Model

Like in the model under conditions of risk we now use assumptions D1 to D10 — D4, D5 and D8 have to be replaced by D4', D5' and D8' — to formulate the model for the determination of the optimal investment date under conditions of uncertainty as a stopping decision model. A general stopped decision process under uncertainty is analyzed by Rieder (1975b). As the investment project is again assumed to be indivisible, the decision process already may be finished before the planning horizon T.

We present this stopping decision model as a dynamic program in the form of the 10–tupel $(I \times Z, K, D, E, \overline{p}, q, w, \beta, g, \mathcal{J}_{T+1})$ of the following meaning:

a) the <u>state space</u> $I \times Z := \{0,1\} \times \mathbf{N}_0^2 \times \mathbf{N} \times \mathbf{R}$. The state $(i,z) = (i,n,y,k,b) \in I \times Z$ consists of three components: 1) $i = 1(0)$ says that in a planning period an (no) opportunity to undertake the project exists. 2) (n,y) is the information state of past investment opportunities defined in assumption D5'. 3) (k,b) is the information state of past market values defined in D4'.

b) the <u>control space</u> $K := \{0,1\}$. If the project is undertaken in the running planning period then $a = 1$. If no investment takes place, then $a = 0$.

c) the <u>set of admissible controls</u> $D : I \to \mathcal{P}(K)$, where $\mathcal{P}$ is the symbol for the power set. We have: $D(0) = \{0\}$, $D(1) = K$.

d) the <u>disturbance space</u> $E := \{0,1\} \times \mathbf{R}$ with generic element $e = (j,r)$. Again $j = 1(0)$ indicates the existence of an (no) investment opportunity and r denotes the market value.

e) the <u>disturbance distributions</u>
   1. $\overline{p}$ is a transition probability (tp) from $\mathbf{N}_0^2$ to $\{0,1\}$ with $\overline{p}(n,y;\{1\}) = p(n,y)$ where $p(n,y)$ is defined in (4,19),
   2. q is a tp from $\mathbf{N} \times \mathbf{R}$ to $\mathbf{R}$; q is given by (4,18).

f) the <u>state transition</u> $w : I \times Z \times K \times E \to I \times Z$ where for $(i,z) = (i,n,y,k,b) \in I \times Z$, $a \in D(i)$ and $e = (j,r) \in E$ we have:

$$w(i,z;a;e) = (j, n+1, y+j, k+1, v(b,r)) \, .$$

The recursion function $v(b,r)$ of the sufficient statistic $b = T(r_{-L}, \dots, r_t)$ is defined in (2.7). It is important to note that v is a nondecreasing function of both coordinates.

g) the <u>discount factor</u> $\beta : K \to [0,1]$ where $\beta(0) = \beta$ and $\beta(1) = 0$. The latter specification means that once the investment is undertaken the decision process is stopped.

h) the <u>one–stage reward function</u> $g : K \times E \to \mathbf{R}$ where

$$g(0,e) \equiv 0 \, ,$$
$$g(1,e) = r - C \quad \text{with} \quad e = (j,r) \in E \, .$$

i) the <u>terminal reward function</u> $\mathcal{J}_{T+1} : I \times Z \to \mathbf{R}$ where according to assumption D10 we have:

$$(4,21) \qquad \text{(I)} \quad \mathcal{J}_{T+1}(i,z) \equiv 0\,, \quad (i,z) \in I \times Z$$

$$(4,22) \qquad \text{(II)} \quad \mathcal{J}_{T+1}(0,z) \equiv 0$$

$$\mathcal{J}_{T+1}(1,z) = N(k,b)\,, \quad z = (n,y,k,b) \in Z\,.$$

(4,21) says that the last possibility for investment is in planning period T, whereas (4,22) indicates that in case of an investment opportunity the project must be undertaken in period $T+1$.

For the following we assume that the posterior expected NPV $N(k,b)$ defined in (4,20) exists. Then the functions $\mathcal{J}_t : I \times Z \to \mathbf{R}$, $1 \le t \le T+1$, where $\mathcal{J}_t(i,z)$ denotes the maximal expected discounted reward from planning period t up to the planning horizon with initial state $(i,z) \in I \times Z$, are well defined. These so–called value function $\mathcal{J}_t$ are recursively computed by means of the value iteration procedure of dynamic programming. $\mathcal{J}_{T+1}$ is given by (4,21) and (4,22), respectively.

For $1 \le t \le T$ and $(i,z) = (i,n,y,k,b) \in I \times Z$ we have:

$$\mathcal{J}_t(0,z) = \beta \int q(k,b;\,dr)[p(n,y)\mathcal{J}_{t+1}(1,n+1,y+1,k+1,v(b,r))$$

$$(4,23) \qquad + (1-p(n,y))\mathcal{J}_{t+1}(0,n+1,y,k+1,v(b,r))]\,,$$

$$(4,24) \qquad \mathcal{J}_t(1,z) = \max\{N(k,b)\,, \mathcal{J}_t(0,z)\}\,.$$

For $1 \le t \le T$ and $(i,z) = (i,n,y,k,b) \in I \times Z$ the optimal investment policy then is characterized by the finite sequence $(f_1,\ldots,f_T)$ of investment decision functions where

$$f_t(0,z) \equiv 0\,,$$

$$(4,25) \qquad f_t(1,z) = \begin{cases} 0 & \text{if} \quad N(k,b) \le \mathcal{J}_t(0,z) \\ 1 & \text{otherwise}\,. \end{cases}$$

The NPV premium $\mathcal{J}_t(0,n,y,k,b)$ describes the value of the project. If the posterior expected NPV $N(k,b)$ is not larger than this value of the project, then the investment project is postponed for at least one more planning period provided the planning horizon has not yet been reached.

4.4.4 Properties of the Optimal Investment Policy

In this section we try to discover structural properties of the optimal investment policy under uncertainty defined by (4,25). We show that the optimal policy is again of control–limit type. This holds not only with respect to the information state (k, b) of the market value but also with regard to the information state (n, y) of the investment opportunity.

But first of all we present an auxiliary result:

LEMMA 4.5. *For all nonincreasing functions $h : \mathbf{R} \to \mathbf{R}$ which are integrable with respect to transition probability q defined in (4,18) we have:*

$$b \to \int q(k, b;\, dr) h(v(b, r)) \quad \text{is nonincreasing},$$

where v is the recursion function of (k, b), nondecreasing in each coordinate.

PROOF. *Remember that q is a monotone transition probability according to Theorem 2.13. Then we have for $b \le b'$:*

$$\int q(k, b;\, dr) h(v(b, r)) \ge \int q(k, b;\, dr) h(v(b', r)) \ge \int q(k, b';\, dr) h(v(b', r)).$$

The second inequality holds because of Theorem 2.7.

Now define for $1 \le t \le T$ and $(i, z) = (i, n, y, k, b) \in I \times Z$:

$$(4,26) \qquad b_t(n, y, k) := \mathrm{Inf}\{b \in \mathbf{R} \mid \mathcal{J}_t(0, z) - N(k, b) \le 0\} \in [-\infty, \infty],$$

where $\mathrm{Inf}\phi := \infty$ and $\mathrm{Inf}\,\mathbf{R} := -\infty$.

Now we are in the position to state the main result, namely the existence of control limits b_t with regard to the information state (k, b):

THEOREM 4.6. *(control limit)*
For $1 \le t \le T$ and $(i, z) = (i, n, y, k, b) \in I \times Z$ we have:

a) $b \to \mathcal{J}_t(i, z) - N(k, b)$ *is nonincreasing,*

b)

$$f_t(1, z) = \begin{cases} 0 & \text{if } b \le b_t(n, y, k) \\ 1 & \text{otherwise}. \end{cases}$$

Proof. *a) We show the monotonicity in b by backward induction. $N(k,b)$ defined in (4,20) is nondecreasing in b because of Theorem 2.13 and because of Theorem 2.7.*

Then $b \to \mathcal{J}_{T+1}(i,z) - N(k,b)$ is clearly nonincreasing. Now assume that a) holds for $t+1 \le \tau \le T+1$. Then we have for period t:

$$\begin{aligned}
&\mathcal{J}_t(0,z) - N(k,b) \\
&= \beta \int q(k,b;\, dr)\{p(n,y)[\mathcal{J}_{t+1}(1,n+1,y+1,k+1,v(b,r)) \\
&- N(k+1,v(b,r))] \\
&+ (1-p(n,y))[\mathcal{J}_{t+1}(0,n+1,y,k+1,v(b,r)) - N(k+1,v(b,r))]\} \\
&+ \beta \int q(k,b;\, dr) N(k+1,v(b,r)) - N(k,b)\,.
\end{aligned}$$

The expression in the curly brackets is nonincreasing in b by the induction hypothesis and by Lemma 4.5.

Using Theorem 2.5 we obtain for the last line: $(\beta-1)N(k,b)$. Because of assumption D4 — $0 < \beta \le 1$ — this is also nonincreasing in b. Therefore, $\mathcal{J}_t(0,z) - N(k,b)$ is nonincreasing with respect to b. Then

$$b \to \mathcal{J}_t(1,z) - N(k,b) = \max\{0, \mathcal{J}_t(0,z) - N(k,b)\}$$

is also nonincreasing.

Part b) of the theorem can immediately be concluded from a) because $N(k,b) \le \mathcal{J}_t(0,z)$ is equivalent to $b \le b_t(n,y,k)$ by (4,25).

Given the information state (n,y) for the opportunity to invest, the quantities $b_t(n,y,k)$ defined in (4,26) in fact turn out to be the <u>control</u> or <u>investment limits</u> with respect to the information state (k,b) of the market value as part b) of the previous theorem shows. Sometimes the $b_t(n,y,k)$ are also referred to as <u>option values</u>.

In this way the control space K is separated into two convex regions with regard to the sufficient statistic $b = T(r_{-L},\ldots,r_t)$: If in planning period t b does not exceed the investment limit $b_t(n,y,k)$, the project is postponed, otherwise it is undertaken in period t. Thereby it is guaranteed that the posterior expected NPV $N(k,b)$ of the project is larger than the <u>NPV premium</u> $\mathcal{J}_t(0,n,y,k,b_t(n,y,k))$.

Thus, the optimal investment policy $(f_1, \ldots, f_T)$ is of control–limit type, that is the optimal investment decision functions f_t are nondecreasing with respect to b.

Now we turn to the information state (n, y) of the investment opportunity by keeping the information state (k, b) with respect to the market value constant. We are again interested in showing the monotonicity of the decision functions f_t in dependence of (n, y).

THEOREM 4.7. *(Monotonicity in (n, y)) Let the terminal reward function (I) from (4,21) be given. Furthermore, let $(n, y), (n', y') \in \mathbb{N}_0^2$ with $(n, y) \leq (n', y')$ by (2,8'), i.e. $y \leq y'$ and $n - y \geq n' - y'$.
Then we have for $1 \leq t \leq T$, $i \in I$ and $z = (n, y, k, b)$, $z' = (n', y', k, b) \in Z$:*

a) $\mathcal{J}_t(i, z) \leq \mathcal{J}_t(i, z')$,
b) $f_t(1, z) \geq f_t(1, z')$ and $b_t(n, y, k) \leq b_t(n', y', k)$.

PROOF. a) *We prove the assertion as usual by backward induction. Remember that $p(n, y) \leq p(n', y')$ by Corollary 2.14.*

For $t = T$ the assertion follows for $\mathcal{J}_{T+1}$ specified by (4,21). Let a) be satisfied for $t + 1 \leq \tau \leq T$; then we have for planning period t:

$$\begin{aligned}
\mathcal{J}_t(0, z) \leq \beta \int & q(k, b;\, dr)[p(n, y)\mathcal{J}_{t+1}(1, n' + 1, y' + 1, k + 1, v(b, r)) \\
& + (1 - p(n, y))\mathcal{J}_{t+1}(0, n' + 1, y', k + 1, v(b, r))] \\
\leq \beta \int & q(k, b;\, dr)\{p(n', y')[\mathcal{J}_{t+1}(1, n' + 1, y' + 1, k + 1, v(b, r)) \\
& - \mathcal{J}_{t+1}(0, n' + 1, y', k + 1, v(b, r))] \\
& + \mathcal{J}_{t+1}(0, n' + 1, y', k + 1, v(b, r))\} \\
& = \mathcal{J}_t(0, z') .
\end{aligned}$$

*The first inequality holds because of the induction hypothesis. The second inequality results from the monotonicity of $p(n, y)$, from $\mathcal{J}_{t+1}(1, n' + 1, y' + 1, \cdot) \geq \mathcal{J}_{t+1}(1, n' + 1, y', \cdot)$ by the induction hypothesis and from
$\mathcal{J}_{t+1}(1, n' + 1, y', \cdot) \geq \mathcal{J}_{t+1}(0, n' + 1, y', \cdot)$ by (4,24).*

*Part b) follows from a) by means of Theorem 4.6 because of
$\mathcal{J}_t(i, z) - N(k, b) \leq \mathcal{J}_t(i, z') - N(k, b)$.*

For given information state (k, b) of the market value part a) of this theorem together with (4,25) implies in each planning period t the existence of an integer $y_t^*(n,k,b) \in \mathbf{N}_0$ of the following meaning: If the sufficient statistic $y = T(M_{-L'}, \ldots, M_t)$ of the opportunities to invest up to period t is not smaller than y_t^* then the project is postponed. If instead y is smaller than y_t^*, then investment takes place in period t.

Theorem 4.7.b) expresses this behaviour by means of the investment limits b_t: If (k, b) is kept constant, then the larger the observed number of investment opportunities is, the more likely the project will be postponed, i.e. $b_t(n, y, k) \leq b_t(n, y', k)$.

A large number of past opportunities causes the investor to believe that there will be a lot of future opportunities to invest up to the planning horizon. And at one of these opportunities the posterior expected NPV of the project possibly will be higher than the current one.

By the way, this result is in accordance with the sensitivity result with respect to p of the investment model under conditions of risk because of the monotonicity property of $p(n, y)$ (cp. Lemma 4.2).

Of course, this monotonicity result with respect to the number of investment opportunities holds only for terminal reward specification (I). In case the investor must undertake the project at the planning horizon, this monotonicity clearly will be destroyed.

4.4.5 The Comparison with Known Models

Roberts/Weitzman (1981) examine $R\&D$ projects. In their model learning takes place at each stage of investment. Thereby the uncertainty about the value of the completed project is reduced. In this case the use of the NPV–rule for such projects might reject investments that should be undertaken.

Contrary, in the models of Cukierman (1980) and Bernanke (1983) uncertainty is resolved by waiting with the acceptance of the project. Both investment models are designed in discrete time and assume a risk–neutral investor, i.e. the utility function is linear with respect to the market parameter. Furthermore, they define the state of the economy and the information state, respectively, in a general way. This state reflects all relevant microeconomic as well as macroeconomic data, like e.g. information about markets and competitors, tax laws but also about economic policies of the government.

Apart from the difficulty to condense these data to a state of the economy in an appropriate way, the three models mentioned are not explicitly based on valuation on the capital market. If the manager of a firm selects the investment projects in this way, this need not be in accordance with the real objective, namely the maximization of the firm value to its owners (stockholders).

In the model of Cukierman (1980) the type of the investment project is already given. The only criterion to distinguish between the projects within this type is a certain feature, e.g. the size of the project. Therefore, at the beginning of the planning process the investor is confronted with a large (infinite) number of different projects. He must decide the size of the project and moreover when to undertake the project. The decision criterion is the NPV which depends not only on the project size but also on an unknown parameter.

At the beginning of the planning process the investor is assumed to know a prior distribution for this unknown parameter. Moreover, in each planning period the investor is able to improve the knowledge about the parameter by observing the state of the economy, whose distribution also depends on the parameter. For that fixed observation cost per period are charged.

The determination of the optimal investment date is only demonstrated for the undiscounted model with normally distributed random variables. This is done without using dynamic programming by computing the optimal myopic investment decision. Thus, the construction date of the project is just optimal with regard to this class of investment policies.

The most essential result concerns the postponement of the investment project if the variance of the prior distribution of the unknown parameter is suitably large. Such irreversible investment projects are postponed or rejected at all. Thereby the demand for reversible projects increases.

Contrary to Cukierman, Bernanke (1983) considers the selection of at most one of a finite number of irreversible investment projects over a finite planning horizon.

The decision is based on the sum of the discounted net cash flows and a salvage value at the planning horizon, which both depend on the respective information state and state of the economy, respectively, of the planning period. The net cash flows of each period as well as the salvage value are assumed to be independent of the project age. In our opinion this assumption seems to be somewhat problematic. For example, this means that given the state of the economy the salvage value of a project undertaken in the first planning period is equal to the salvage value of a project invested in period T. Cukierman (1980) makes the same kind of assumption but compensates the loss from foregone new cash flows arising from the postponement of the project by charging information cost.

The number of Bernanke's information states is finite. The information state is assumed to evolve according to a Markov chain which can arise from a Bayesian learning process. Like in our model the optimal investment policy is of control–limit type with properties that are characteristic for investment in irreversible projects: On the one hand, the optimal policy is not myopic — later on we will discuss a special case of our model where the myopic policy is optimal. On the other hand, contrary to the NPV rule for investment in reversible projects, investing in an irreversible project requires that additionally the NPV premium must be earned. In other words: If a reversible project is advantageous, we must not conclude that its irreversible counterpart is advantageous, too.

Bernanke denotes the optimal investment policy as "bad news principle" for the following reason: If in planning period t the project is not undertaken and therefore the new cash flow at t is foregone, the investor still has the option to make the commitment in period $t+1$. The decision to invest in period t first of all complies with "bad news" in period $t+1$, which would justify to undertake the project immediately and as a consequence to abandon the option (cp. Bernanke (1983), pp. 91).

But there exists also the possibility that in planning period $t+1$ "good news" occur instead of "bad news". If in period t the information state is not very promising, the investor maintains the option for committing the project at least to period $t+1$ in hope for better information states.

Whereas we are dealing with the question when to buy a real asset, Venezia (1983) determines the optimal date for selling an asset under conditions of uncertainty. If the cash flow obtained from selling the asset follows a Normal distribution, Venezia compares the Bayesian approach with the non– Bayesian decision rule.

After this brief review of Bernanke's model we of course have to pose the question for the differences to our investment timing model under conditions of uncertainty. First of all we mention the consistence of the NPV of the project with the capital market equilibrium. In this way it is possible to estimate the parameters of the market value distribution, which are assumed to be known, by means of sample data. Besides these "hard" data we also use "soft" data in form of a prior distribution for the unknown parameter of the market value distribution in order to compute the posterior distribution of the market value by means of Bayes'Theorem. This explicit description of the probability structure is used to prove the monotonicity of the value functions and thus the existence of a control-limit policy.

With that we derive qualitative properties of the optimal investment policy. This is done in the next section.

4.4.6 Sensitivity Analyses

This section deals with sensitivity investigations with respect to the capital cost of the project, the planning horizon, the discount factor and the prior distributions. Furthermore, we compare the optimal investment policy with the certainty equivalence policy which results from replacing the random variables by their posterior expected values. This is all done on the basis of the investment limits (4,26) and the so defined optimal investment decisions from Theorem 4.6.b).

We choose the following procedure and notation: We always specify one parameter of the model with two different values, e.g. an investment project with capital cost C_1 and another one with capital cost C_2 where $C_1 < C_2$ is assumed to hold. The corresponding value functions are denoted by $\mathcal{J}_t^1$ and $\mathcal{J}_t^2$, the control limits by b_t^1 and b_t^2 and the optimal investment decision functions by f_t^1 and f_t^2.

Moreover we denote the posterior expected NPV $N(k,b)$ from (4,20) by N^1 and N^2.

4.4.6.1 Variation of the Capital Cost

First we investigate the effects on the optimal investment behaviour by changing the capital cost of the project. For that purpose we compare two investment projects differing only in the capital cost C_1 and C_2, respectively. We assume that $C_1 < C_2$ holds.

THEOREM 4.8. *For $1 \leq t \leq T$ and $(i,z) = (i,n,y,k,b) \in I \times Z$ we have:*

a) $\mathcal{J}_t^1(i,z) - N^1(k,b) \leq \mathcal{J}_t^2(i,z) - N^2(k,b)$,

b) $f_t^1(1,z) \geq f_t^2(1,z)$ *and* $b_t^1(n,y,k) \leq b_t^2(n,y,k)$.

PROOF. *Part a) is shown by backward induction. For $t = T$ the assertion for the terminal reward specification (I) from (4,21) follows immediately.*

For (II) from (4,22) we have by means of Theorem 2.5:

$$\begin{aligned}\mathcal{J}_T^1(0,z) - N^1(k,b) &= [\beta p(n,y) - 1][\int q(k,b;\,dr)r - C_1]\\ &\le [\beta p(n,y) - 1][\int q(k,b;\,dr)r - C_2]\\ &= \mathcal{J}_T^2(0,z) - N^2(k,b)\,.\end{aligned}$$

Consequently, $\mathcal{J}_T^1(1,z) - N^1(k,b) \le \mathcal{J}_T^2(1,z) - N^2(k,b)$ *also holds.*

Then we have for planning period t:

$$\begin{aligned}&\mathcal{J}_t^1(0,z) - N^1(k,b)\\ &= \beta p(n,y) \int q(k,b;\,dr)[\mathcal{J}_{t+1}^1(1,n+1,y+1,k+1,v(b,r))\\ &- N^1(k+1,v(b,r))]\\ &+ \beta(1-p(n,y)) \int q(k,b;\,dr)[\mathcal{J}_{t+1}^1(0,n+1,y,k+1,v(b,r))\\ &- N^1(k+1,v(b,r))]\\ &+ \beta \int q(k,b;\,dr)E(k+1,v(b,r)) - E(k,b) + (1-\beta)C_1\\ &\le \mathcal{J}_t^2(0,z) - N^2(k,b)\,,\end{aligned}$$

where $E(k,b) := \int q(k,b;\,dr)r$.

The inequality holds because of the induction hypothesis and the assumption that the discount factor β is not greater than one.

As easily can be seen part a) is also true for $i = 1$.
Part b) of the theorem then follows from a) by means of Theorem 4.6.

Theorem 4.8 says that high capital cost C of the project imply also high control limits b_t. The more expensive the irreversible investment project is, the more carefully the investor decides its commitment which is expressed by a comparable later investment date.

4.4.6.2 Variation of the Riskless Interest Rate

Now we are interested in the effects on the optimal investment decisions if the riskless interest rate m or equivalently the discount factor β is changed. The result is then compared with that of the deterministic static and dynamic investment models. We specify two discount factors β_1 and β_2 with $\beta_1 \le \beta_2$.

THEOREM 4.9. *Let the terminal reward function be given by* (4,21), *i.e.* $\mathcal{J}_{T+1}(\cdot) \equiv 0$.
Then we have for $1 \leq t \leq T$ *and* $(i,z) = (i,n,y,k,b) \in I \times Z$:

a) $\mathcal{J}_t^1(i,z) \leq \mathcal{J}_t^2(i,z)$,
b) $f_t^1(1,z) \geq f_t^2(1,z)$ *and* $b_t^1(n,y,k) \leq b_t^2(n,y,k)$.

PROOF. *From* $\mathcal{J}_{T+1}^1(i,z) = \mathcal{J}_{T+1}^2(i,z) = \mathcal{J}_{T+1}(i,z) \equiv 0$ *we obtain by backward induction that* $\mathcal{J}_t^1(i,z) \geq 0$ *and* $\mathcal{J}_t^2(i,z) \geq 0$, $1 \leq t \leq T$. *The validity of assertion a) then results from the definition of the value functions* (4,23) *and* (4,24). *Part b) again is an immediate consequence of a).*

Form the preceding theorem we see that an increase of the discount factor leads to an increase of the investment limits b_t and thereby to a postponement of the project. But this is only true if at the planning horizon there is no more opportunity to invest, i.e. in the case of terminal reward specification (I) from (4,21).

Contrary, if the project must be undertaken at the planning horizon provided an opportunity exists (specification (II) from (4,22)), losses can occur in case the posterior expected NPV $N(k,b)$ is negative. If in this situation the investor would behave according to the above theorem, low opportunity cost of capital of the project m_p would imply a late date for investment, possibly the planning horizon. We have previously described the possible consequences. In this framework it can be advantageous for the investor to put the capital cost C into an alternative (financial) asset although the opportunity cost of capital m_p are low.

Now we turn back to the assertion of the theorem that a high discount rate implies high option values. Then it is more likely that the investment project is postponed. But we want to analyze the change of the investment decision by variation of the riskless interest rate (market interest rate) m. By assumption D10 the discount factor β is determined by the opportunity cost of capital of the project m_p, namely $\beta = 1/(1+m_p)$. m_p itself is defined in (4,9):

$$m_p = \lambda m_c + (1-\lambda)m\,,$$

where λ is the risk parameter of the project and m_c denotes the company cost of capital.

First suppose that the investment project under consideration is <u>less risky</u> than the existing business of the firm, i.e. $\lambda < 1$. Then an increase of the market interest rate m implies also an increase of the project cost of capital m_p. In this case a low market interest rate m leads to high investment limits b_t, perhaps this means the postponement of the project. Remember that by assumption the capital cost C is not invested at the interest rate m before the project is undertaken. If m is high, a late commitment of the project would mean high losses of interest earnings. Thus, it is advantageous not to delay the investment.

If the investment project is riskier than the existing business of the firm, i.e. $\lambda > 1$, an increase of the market interest rate m leads to a decrease of the project cost of capital m_p. In this case the higher the market interest rate m is, the higher are the investment limits. Then the project would be postponed. This sensitivity result is in accordance with traditional investment theory saying that higher interest rates discourage investment. The same holds also for the deterministic dynamic investment model from section 4.2. If the net cash flows are independent of the project age, we know from section 4.2.2 that higher market interest rates increase the value of the option to invest at a future date.

There are two opposing forces at work when looking at investment as a dynamic process. On the one hand, in case of a low risk project compared to the existing business of the firm, the "time preference" effect dominates. This result — a low market interest rate m leads to a high NPV premium — is also obtained by Mc Donald/Siegel (1986). On the other hand, for a high risk project an increase of the market interest rate implies an increase of the NPV premium via a decrease of the opportunity cost of capital m_p of the project. This low "rate of return" m_p discourages the investor from undertaking the project. Here a kind of "risk preference" effect dominates.

Like in our model, in the arbitrage–based model of Heaney and Jones the effect of changing m also is not definitely determined but decisively depends on the risk parameter of the project as well as on other parameters of the model (cp. Heaney/Jones (1988), chapter 4).

4.4.6.3 Variation of the Planning Horizon

The next sensitivity investigation is concerned with the effects of a change of the planning horizon and connected with that of the economic life of the project on the optimal investment dates.

We start from two different planning horizons T_1 and T_1 with $T_1 < T_2$ and assume without loss of generality that $T_1 := T$ and $T_2 := T + 1$.

Also here the sensitivity result only holds in the case that at the planning horizon there is no opportunity for investment.

THEOREM 4.10. *Let the terminal reward function be specified by* (4,21), *i.e.* $\mathcal{J}^1_{T+1}(\cdot) = \mathcal{J}^2_{T+2}(\cdot) \equiv 0$.
Then we have for $1 \le t \le T$ *and* $(i,z) = (i,n,y,k,b) \in I \times Z$:

a) $\mathcal{J}^1_t(i,z) \le \mathcal{J}^2_t(i,z)$
b) $f^1_t(1,z) \ge f^2_t(1,z)$ *and* $b^1_t(n,y,k) \le b^2_t(n,y,k)$.

PROOF. a) *We have for planning period* $T+1$:

$$\mathcal{J}^1_{T+1}(0,z) = \mathcal{J}^2_{T+1}(0,z) \equiv 0 \quad \text{and}$$

$$\mathcal{J}^1_{T+1}(1,z) \equiv 0 \le \max\{N(k,b),0\} = \mathcal{J}^2_{T+1}(1,z).$$

Therefore assertion a) *can be proved by backward induction whereas part* b) *easily can be concluded from* a).

Given the information state $z \in Z$, a larger planning horizon increases the NPV premiums $\mathcal{J}_t(0,\cdot)$ as well as the investment limits b_t. The more planning periods the investor has available to undertake the project, the longer he waits with its commitment. Or in terms of the project life: A long economic life of the project means that the investor has to live with it for a long time. Consequently he chooses the optimal investment date more carefully which is expressed by a possibly later commitment of the project.

This result is in accordance with that of the model under conditions of risk from section 4.3 (cp. Lemma 4.3).

4.4.6.4 Variation of the Prior Distributions

Until now the sensitivity investigations have been restricted to economic parameters of the model, namely the capital cost, the market interst rate and the project life. In the following we deal with the effects on the optimal investment decisions if the stochastics are changed. We vary the a priori distributions of the unknown probability of an investment opportunity and of the unknown parameter of the distribution of the market value.

Before this can be done we must agree upon how to compare two prior distributions. We make this comparison be means of the so–called monotone likelihood ratio (MLR), which already has been introduced in chapter

2. In Definition 2.9 we consider the MLR for the family of probability distributions of the sufficient statistic Y.

Now we need the MLR to compare two prior distributions, namely the prior distributions $\overline{\mu}_r^1$ and $\overline{\mu}_r^2$ of the unknown parameter θ of the market value distribution and the prior distributions $\overline{\mu}_p^1$ and $\overline{\mu}_p^2$ of the unknown probability parameter of an investment opportunity in a planning period.

We start from the respective density functions of the prior distributions.

DEFINITION 4.11. *Let two density functions* $h_1, h_2 : D \to (0, \infty), D \subseteq \mathbf{R}$, *be given. We say that the pair* (h_1, h_2) *has a monotone likelihood ratio (MLR), denoted by* $h_1 \prec h_2$, *if* $\theta \to h_2(\theta)/h_1(\theta)$ *is nondecreasing.*

In the following we give a characterization of the MLR–property (cp. e.g. Eaton (1982), Theorem 3.2). In this way we see that the two distributions are related by first order stochastic dominance.

LEMMA 4.12. *Let two density functions* $h_1, h_2 : D \to (0, \infty), D \subseteq \mathbf{R}$, *be given. Then we have for all nondecreasing functions* $g : D \to \mathbf{R}$ *for which the following integrals exists:*

$$h_1 \prec h_2 \quad \textit{implies} \quad \int g(\theta)h_1(\theta)\,d\theta \leq \int g(\theta)h_2(\theta)\,d\theta\,.$$

In the next two sections we perform the sensitivity investigations with regard to the previously mentioned prior distributions. After that we illustrate the general results by the specification of concrete probability distributions.

4.4.6.4.1 The Distribution of the Market Value

We are interested in the effects on the optimal investment decisions by a change of the market value distribution; more specifically we vary the prior distribution $\overline{\mu}_r$ of the unknown parameter of the market value distribution.

For that we consider two prior distributions $\overline{\mu}_r^1$ and $\overline{\mu}_r^2$ which are represented by the density functions h_r^1 and h_r^2.

THEOREM 4.13. *Let* h_r^1 *and* h_r^2 *be two density functions for the unknown parameter* $\theta \in \mathbf{R}$ *of the market value distribution* ν_θ *and assume that* $h_r^1 \prec h_r^2$, *i.e. the pair* (h_r^1, h_r^2) *has a MLR.*

If ν_θ is the Gamma distribution, we have for $1 \le t \le T$ and $(i,z) = (i,n,y,k,b) \in I \times Z$:

a) $\mathcal{J}_t^1(i,z) - N^1(k,b) \le \mathcal{J}_t^2(i,z) - N^2(k,b)$,
b) $f_t^1(1,z) \ge f_t^2(1,z)$ and $b_t^1(n,y,k) \le b_t^2(n,y,k)$.

If ν_θ is the Normal and the Lognormal distribution, respectively, then in a) and b) the reversed inequalities hold.

PROOF. *We prove the assertion only for the Gamma distribution. Let*

$$h_j(k,b;\theta) := g(k,b;\theta)h_\tau^j(\theta) / \int g(k,b;\theta')h_\tau^j(\theta')\,d\theta'$$

be the density function of the posterior distribution of the unknown parameter θ from (4,17) for the prior density h_τ^j, $j = 1,2$.

Then we have for every information state (k,b) $h_1(k,b;\cdot) \prec h_2(k,b;\cdot)$ because of $h_\tau^1 \prec h_\tau^2$.

We know from Lemma 2.12 that $\theta \to \nu_\theta(B)$ is nonincreasing for all increasing sets $B \subseteq \mathbf{R}^+$.

Now denote the posterior market value distribution, defined in (4,18), for the prior density h_τ^j by

$$q_j(k,b;B) := \int \nu_\theta(B) h_j(k,b;\,\theta)\,d\theta\,, \quad j = 1,2\,.$$

Then by means of Lemma 4.12 we have $q_1(k,b;B) \ge q_2(k,b;B)$. But this just means that for every information state (k,b) the posterior distribution q_1 stochastically dominates the posterior distribution q_2. Consequently we have $N^1(k,b) \ge N^2(k,b)$.

After these preliminaries we are in the position to prove assertion a) by backward induction. Let $t = T+1$. Then we have for the terminal reward specification (I) from (4,21): $-N^1(k,b) \le -N^2(k,b)$.
In case of (II) from (4,22) for $i = 0$ the same inequality results whereas for $i = 1$ both difference functions are equal to zero.

Let a) *be satisfied for* $t+1 \leq \tau \leq T+1$; *then we have for period* t:

$$\begin{aligned}
&\mathcal{J}_t^1(0,z) - N^1(k,b) \\
&\leq \beta \int q_1(k,b;\, dr)\{p(n,y)[\mathcal{J}_{t+1}^2(1,n+1,y+1,k+1,b+r) \\
&- N^2(k+1,b+r)] \\
&+ (1-p(n,y))[\mathcal{J}_{t+1}^2(0,n+1,y,k+1,b+r) - N^2(k+1,b+r)]\} \\
&+ (\beta-1)N^2(k,b) \\
&\leq \mathcal{J}_t^2(0,z) - N^2(k,b)\,.
\end{aligned}$$

The first inequality holds because of the induction hypothesis and because of $\beta \leq 1$. *The second inequality is valid because* q_2 *is dominated by* q_1 *and the difference functions* $\mathcal{J}_{t+1} - N$ *are nonincreasing in* b *according to Theorem 4.6.a). It is easy to check that* a) *is also true for* $i = 1$. *Again assertion* b) *is an immediate consequence of part* a).

We mentioned that for the Normal and the Lognormal distribution the theorem holds with the inequalities reversed. The reason is that for these distributions $\theta \to \nu_\theta(B)$ is nondecreasing for increasing sets B by Lemma 2.12.

4.4.6.4.2 The Investment Opportunities

Now we investigate the sensitivity of the optimal investment policy if the prior distribution $\overline{\mu}_p$ of the unknown probability p which indicates that in a planning period an opportunity for investment occurs is varied. We consider also in this case two prior distributions $\overline{\mu}_p^1$ and $\overline{\mu}_p^2$ which are characterized by the density functions h_p^1 and h_p^2.

THEOREM 4.14. *Let the terminal reward function be given by* (4,21), *i.e.* $\mathcal{J}_{T+1}(\cdot) \equiv 0$. *Furthermore, let* h_p^1 *and* h_p^2 *be density functions for the unknown probability* $p \in (0,1]$ *and assume that* $h_p^1 \prec h_p^2$, *i.e. the pair* (h_p^1, h_p^2) *has a MLR.*
Then we have for $1 \leq t \leq T$ *and* $(i,z) = (i,n,y,k,b) \in I \times Z$:

a) $\mathcal{J}_t^1(i,z) \leq \mathcal{J}_t^2(i,z)$,
b) $f_t^1(1,z) \geq f_t^2(1,z)$ and $b_t^1(n,y,k) \leq b_t^2(n,y,k)$.

PROOF. *Given the information state* (n,y) *the posterior probability of an opportunity to invest for prior density* h_p^j, $j = 1,2$, *by* (4,19) *is:*

$$p_j(n,y) = \int_0^1 \pi^{y+1}(1-\pi)^{n-y} h_p^j(\pi)\,d\pi \Big/ \int_0^1 \pi^y(1-\pi)^{n-y} h_p^j(\pi)\,d\pi\,.$$

Because of $h_p^1 \prec h_p^2$ we conclude from Definition 4.11 and Lemma 4.12: $p_1(n,y) \leq p_2(n,y)$.

Now the proof of assertion a) can be accomplished like the one of Theorem 4.7.a) and assertion b) again results from a).

If we compare this sensitivity result with the same one for the investment model under conditions of risk (Lemma 4.2), we notice that now this result is only obtained for $\mathcal{J}_{T+1}(\cdot) \equiv 0$. But in the model under risk we have been able to perform the sensitivity analysis also for the case that at the planning horizon the project must be undertaken provided an opportunity for investment exists. We had to impose the condition that the "expected NPV" is not negative, i.e. $\int r q(dr) \geq C$ (see assumption D8).

The equivalent condition in the model under conditions of uncertainty would be $N(k,b) \geq 0$, i.e. for each information state (k,b) the posterior expected NPV had to be nonnegative — an extremely unrealistic assumption which therefore has been renounced.

4.4.6.4.3 Illustrative Examples

After the theoretical analysis of the preceding sections it is time to illustrate the content of relation "$\prec$" from Definition 4.11 by the specification of concrete distributions. We start with the market value distribution ν_θ which first is assumed to be the Gamma- $G(\alpha,\theta)$ –distribution. The prior distribution of the unknown parameter θ is chosen as the natural conjugate Gamma $-G(\gamma,\delta)$–distribution. Then we have $E(\theta) = \gamma/\delta$ and $\mathrm{Var}(\theta) = \gamma/\delta^2$.

Given two prior Gamma densities $G(\gamma_1,\delta_1)$ and $G(\gamma_2,\delta_2)$, $h_r^1 \prec h_r^2$ is satisfied if $\gamma_1 \leq \gamma_2$ and/or $\delta_1 \geq \delta_2$ holds.

For information state (k,b) the posterior expected market value for density h_r^j is

$$E_j(k,b) := \alpha(\delta_j + b)/(k\alpha + \gamma_j - 1)\,, \quad j = 1,2\,.$$

Now suppose that the $L+1$ market values observed before the beginning of the planning process result in the sufficient statistic b. Then we immediately see:

$$E_1(L+1,b) \geq E_2(L+1,b) \quad \text{if} \quad \gamma_1 > \max\{0, 1-(L+1)\alpha\}\,.$$

Furthermore, we have:

$$\mathrm{Var}(\theta_1) = \gamma_1/\delta_1 \leq \gamma_2/\delta_2 = \mathrm{Var}(\theta_2)\,.$$

In summary we can point out: In case of natural conjugate Gamma distributions, the relation $h_\tau^1 \prec h_\tau^2$ means that density function h_τ^2 contains worse prior information than density h_τ^1. On the one hand, the expected market value $E_2(L+1,b)$ before beginning the planning process is lower than $E_1(L+1,b)$. On the other hand, the variance $\text{Var}(\theta_2)$ of the prior distribution is larger than $\text{Var}(\theta_1)$.

Now we turn to normally distributed market values, i.e. ν_θ is specified as the $N(\theta,\sigma^2)$–distribution. The unknown expectation θ is also assumed to follow a Normal–$N(\mu,\tau^2)$– distribution.

Given two normally distributed prior density functions $N(\mu_1,\tau^2)$ and $N(\mu_2,\tau^2)$, $h_\tau^1 \prec h_\tau^2$ is fulfilled if $\mu_1 \leq \mu_2$ holds.

If before the beginning of the planning process the information state $(L+1,b)$ has been obtained, we have for the expected market value from Table 2.2:

$$\begin{aligned}\mu_1(L+1,b) &= (\tau^2 b + \sigma^2\mu_1)/(\tau^2(L+1)+\sigma^2)\\ &\leq (\tau^2 b + \sigma^2\mu_2)/(\tau^2(L+1)+\sigma^2)\\ &= \mu_2(L+1,b)\,.\end{aligned}$$

In this case density function h_τ^1 expresses worse prior information than density h_τ^2: Before the start of the planning process the expected market value $\mu_1(L+1,b)$ is smaller than $\mu_2(L+1,b)$. The same statement applies for lognormally distributed market values instead of the here used Normal distribution.

With this interpretation the assertion of Theorem 4.13.b) becomes evident. Bad prior information before the beginning of the decision process represented by prior density h_τ^2 in case of the Gamma distribution and represented by prior density h_τ^1 in case of the Normal and the Lognormal distribution implies high investment limits. The riskier the initial position of the investor is, the more carefully he behaves when deciding to undertake the irreversible project.

Finally we briefly illustrate the effect of varying the prior distribution of the unknown probability for an opportunity to invest in a planning period.

For that we suppose that the prior distribution is the natural conjugate Beta–$B(\gamma,\delta)$–distribution. For two prior densities $B(\gamma_1,\delta_1)$ and $B(\gamma_2,\delta_2)$ the relation $h_p^1 \prec h_p^2$ is satisfied if $\gamma_1 \leq \gamma_2$ and/or $\delta_1 \geq \delta_2$ holds.

Then the posterior probability for an investment opportunity for density h_p^j is according to Table 2.2

$$p_j(n,y) = (\gamma_j + y)/(\gamma_j + \delta_j + n), \quad j = 1,2.$$

In case of no prior information, i.e. $(n,y) = (0,0)$ we have $p_1(0,0) \leq p_2(0,0)$.

Thus, the better at the start of the planning process the subjective beliefs of the investor with regard to opportunities for undertaking the project are, the more he can afford to be selective. In Theorem 4.14.b) this is expressed by high investment limits b_t^2 in case of the prior density h_p^2.

We once again draw the attention to the fact that this sensitivity result only holds for the case that at the planning horizon there is no possibility for the commitment. As just mentioned, a high prior probability for an investment opportunity possibly leads to the postponement of the construction date. But this is true for each information state (k,b) concerning the market value. Consequently, in case of the terminal reward function (II) losses are quite possible if the project has to be undertaken at the planning horizon. Therefore, Theorem 4.14 does not apply if at the beginning of period $T+1$ it must be invested, provided there exists such an opportunity.

4.4.6.5 The Certainty Equivalence Policy

One reason for the frequent use of deterministic models in practice is that random quantities are replaced by their expected values. This procedure leads to the so-called certainty equivalence policy. Apart from some special cases, of course, the optimal control policy cannot be calculated in this way (cp. for this subject e.g. Bertsekas (1976), pp. 70).

We compare the optimal investment policy defined by (4,23) — (4,25) and by Theorem 4.6 with the previously described certainty equivalence policy. This latter policy is obtained if in the value functions (4,23) and (4,24) the random market value r is replaced by the posterior expected market value for information state (k,b)

$$E(k,b) := \int q(k,b;\, dr)r\,.$$

To ease the analysis we restrict ourselves to the situation that at the planning horizon no more opportunity for investment exists. The resulting value functions are distinguished from that in (4,23) and (4,24) by the superscript "C". The same convention is applied for the corresponding decision functions.

Then we have for $(i,z) = (i,n,y,k,b) \in I \times Z$:

$$\mathcal{J}_{T+1}^{C}(i,z) \equiv 0\,,$$

and for $1 \leq t \leq T$:

$$\begin{aligned}\mathcal{J}_t^C(0,z) = \beta[&p(n,y)\mathcal{J}_{t+1}^C(1,n+1,y+1,k+1,\overline{v}(k,b))\\ &+(1-p(n,y))\mathcal{J}_{t+1}^C(0,n+1,y,k+1,\overline{v}(k,b))]\end{aligned}$$

where $\overline{v}(k,b) := v(b, E(k,b))$,

$$\mathcal{J}_t^C(1,z) = \max\{N(k,b), \mathcal{J}_t^C(0,z)\}\,.$$

Remember that by (4,20) $N(k,b) = E(k,b) - C$.

Then the certainty equivalence policy is a finite sequence $(f_1^C, \ldots, f_T^C)$ of functions $f_t^C : I \times Z \to \{0,1\}$ where $f_t^C(0,z) \equiv 0$ and

$$f_t^C(1,z) = \begin{cases} 0 & \text{if } \; N(k,b) \leq \mathcal{J}_t^C(0,z) \\ 1 & \text{otherwise}\,. \end{cases}$$

First we show that the certainty equivalence policy is also of control–limit type. Let for $(i,z) = (i,n,y,k,b) \in I \times Z$ and $1 \leq t \leq T$:

$$b_t^C(n,y,k) := \mathrm{Inf}\{b \in \mathbf{R} \mid \mathcal{J}_t^C(0,z) - N(k,b) \leq 0\}\,.$$

LEMMA 4.15. *For $(i,z) = (i,n,y,k,b) \in I \times Z$ let $E(k+1,\overline{v}(k,b)) = E(k,b)$.*
Then we have for $1 \leq t \leq T$:

a) *$b \to \mathcal{J}_t^C(i,z) - N(k,b)$ is nonincreasing,*

b)

$$f_t^C(1,z) = \begin{cases} 0 & \textit{if } \; b \leq b_t^C(n,y,k) \\ 1 & \textit{otherwise} \end{cases}$$

PROOF. *In order to prove assertion a) remember that $q(k,b;\cdot)$ is a monotone transition probability by Theorem 2.13 and consequently $b \to N(k,b)$ is nondecreasing by Theorem 2.7. Therefore, the beginning of the backward induction for $t = T$ is assured.*

Then we have for period t using $E(k+1,\overline{v}(k,b)) = E(k,b)$:

$$\begin{aligned}\mathcal{J}_t^C(0,z) - N(k,b) = \beta\{&p(n,y)[\mathcal{J}_{t+1}^C(1,n+1,y+1,k+1,\overline{v}(k,b))\\ &- N(k+1,\overline{v}(k,b))]\\ &+(1-p(n,y))[\mathcal{J}_{t+1}^C(0,n+1,y,k+1,\overline{v}(k,b))\\ &- N(k+1,\overline{v}(k,b))]\\ &+(\beta-1)N(k,b)\end{aligned}$$

Because of the induction hypothesis and as $\beta \leq 1$, this difference function is nonincreasing in b. The same holds for $\mathcal{J}_t^C(1,z) - N(k,b)$. Part b) is an easy consequence of a) because $N(k,b) \leq \mathcal{J}_t^C(0,z)$ is equivalent to $b \leq b_t^C(n,y,k)$.

The assumption $E(k+1,\overline{v}(k,b)) = E(k,b)$ just made in the lemma is familiar to us from the binary portfolio model under conditions of uncertainty. It is fulfilled for the continuous distributions of Table 2.2 together with the respective natural conjugate prior distribution (see Corollary 3.14 and the following remarks).

In order to be able to compare the optimal investment policy with the certainty equivalence policy we need the following auxiliary result:

LEMMA 4.16. *For $(i,z) = (i,n,y,k,b) \in I \times Z$ let $b \to E(k,b)$ and $v(b,r)$ be affine functions. Then we have for $1 \leq t \leq T$ that $b \to \mathcal{J}_t^C(i,z)$ is convex.*

PROOF. *For proving the assertion we use basic properties of convex functions which e.g. can be found in Elster et al. (1977), pp. 68.*
$\mathcal{J}_T^C(0,z) \equiv 0$ and $\mathcal{J}_T^C(1,z) = \max\{N(k,b),0\}$ is convex in b.

Let the assertion be true for $t+1 \leq \tau \leq T$. Then $\mathcal{J}_{t+1}^C(i,n,y,k+1,\overline{v}(k,b))$ is also a convex function with respect to b because $b \to \overline{v}(k,b)$ is affine. As a consequence, $b \to \mathcal{J}_t^C(\cdot)$ is convex, too.

This leads to the following sensitivity result:

Theorem 4.17. *For $(i,z) = (i,n,y,k,b) \in I \times Z$ let $b \to E(k,b)$ and $v(b,r)$ be affine functions.*
Then we have for $1 \le t \le T$:

a) $\mathcal{J}_t^C(i,z) \le \mathcal{J}_t(i,z)$,

b) $f_t^C(1,z) \ge f_t(1,z)$ and $b_t^C(n,y,k) \le b_t(n,y,k)$.

Proof. a) *The proof goes by backward induction.*
Then we have: $\mathcal{J}_T^C(0,z) = \mathcal{J}_T(0,z) \equiv 0$ and

$$\mathcal{J}_T^C(1,z) = \mathcal{J}_T(1,z) = \max\{N(k,b),0\}.$$

Assume that the assertion holds for $t+1 \le \tau \le T$. For period t we have:

$$\begin{aligned}\mathcal{J}_t(0,z) &\ge \beta \int q(k,b;\,dr)[p(n,y)\mathcal{J}_{t+1}^C(1,n+1,y+1,k+1,v(b,r)) \\ &\qquad + (1-p(n,y))\mathcal{J}_{t+1}^C(0,n+1,y,k+1,v(b,r))] \\ &\ge \beta[p(n,y)\mathcal{J}_{t+1}^C(1,n+1,y+1,k+1,\overline{v}(k,b)) \\ &\qquad + (1-p(n,y))\mathcal{J}_{t+1}^C(0,n+1,y,k+1,\overline{v}(k,b))] \\ &= \mathcal{J}_t^C(0,z)\end{aligned}$$

The first inequality follows from the induction hypothesis, the second is established by Lemma 4.16 and by means of Jensen's inequality.

$$\begin{aligned}\mathcal{J}_t(1,z) &= \max\{N(k,b)\,,\mathcal{J}_t(0,z)\} \\ &\ge \max\{N(k,b)\,,\mathcal{J}_t^C(0,z)\} = \mathcal{J}_t^C(1,z)\,.\end{aligned}$$

Part b) of the theorem again follows from a).

Before we are going to give an interpretation of this sensitivity result we want to clarify for what distributions the assumptions of the preceding theorem are satisfied. If the market value distribution ν_θ is the Gamma $-G(\alpha,\theta)$–distribution and the prior distribution for θ is the conjugate $G(\gamma,\delta)$–distribution, we have $E(k,b) = \alpha(\delta+b)/(k\alpha+\gamma-1)$.

If the market value distribution as well as the prior distribution are Normal distributions, we have from Table 2.2

$$E(k,b) = \mu(k,b) = (\tau^2 b + \sigma^2 \mu)/(\tau^2 k + \sigma^2)\,.$$

In both cases the recursion function is given by $v(b, r) = b + r$. Consequently, $E(k, \cdot)$ and v are affine functions.

The result of the sensitivity analysis stated in Theorem 4.17 is as expected: The "certainty equivalence" — investor tends to undertake the project earlier than the investor who behaves optimally. This is not surprising because the CE–investor ignores the estimation risk by replacing the random market value by the posterior expected market value. This procedure can be interpreted in such a way that the CE–investor assumes to be perfectly informed, which is expressed by the one–point distribution $E(k, b)$ for the market value. Then this result is in accordance with the sensitivity result for the variation of the prior distribution for the unknown parameter θ of the market value distribution (see Theorem 4.13): The less risky the initial information of the investor is, the earlier the irreversible investment project will be undertaken.

4.4.7 The Optimal Exercise Date of an American Call Option

In the introductory remarks to this chapter we have noted that the model for the determination of the optimal investment date under conditions of uncertainty is not only well suited for real irreversible projects but also for a special kind of financial asset. Namely this model also can be used to compute the optimal exercise date of an American call option under the restrictive assumption that the owner cannot sell the option on the secondary market.

The buyer of an option has to pay a certain price which is determined by the market. An American (European) call option gives its owner the right to buy stock at a specified exercise price C on or before (on) the specified expiration date T or to let it expire unexercised.

Whereas most of the literature in this field is concerned with the valuation of options, i.e. with the determination of the price of the option, we instead assume that the price has already been specified and also has been paid. We are then only interested in the question when it is optimal to exercise the American call option during its time to maturity. But this point is of no relevance in modern option pricing theory which has been initiated by Black/Scholes (1973). With the assumptions made there it is never optimal to exercise the option before its expiration date (cp. for these assumptions e.g. Uhlir/ Steiner (1986), pp. 181 and pp. 198).

Besides from our discrete–time framework the main difference between our investment model and the Black/Scholes–model is that we do not allow the owner of the call option to invest the exercise price C at the riskless interest rate m until the exercise. This difference is the reason that in our model it is in general optimal to exercise the option before its expiration date.

In order to derive the optimal exercise date we have to simplify the model introduced in section 4.3.3 a little bit. Now the market value r of the investment is specified as the price of the stock on which the call option is written. Like in the Black/Scholes–model we also assume that during the maturity time of the option there are no dividend payments on the stock. Furthermore, the owner of the option can in principle buy stock at one of the T dates $1,\ldots,T$ at the specified exercise price C. As in this case in each planning period an opportunity exists to invest, the state of the model is reduced by the tripel (i,n,y) just to (k,b) because we have $p(n,y) \equiv 1$. The owner of the option also cannot be forced to buy the stock at the expiration date. Hence, we only have to consider the terminal reward function (I) given by (4,21).

Then the so modified stopping decision model is characterized by the following set of value functions (compare with (4,23) and (4,24)):

$$\mathcal{J}_{T+1}(k,b) \equiv 0\,,$$

and for $1 \leq t \leq T$:

$$\mathcal{J}_t^0(k,b) = \beta \int q(k,b;\, dr)\mathcal{J}_{t+1}(k+1, v(b,r))\,, \tag{4,27}$$

$$\mathcal{J}_t^1(k,b) = N(k,b)\,, \tag{4,28}$$

$$\mathcal{J}_t(k,b) = \max\{N(k,b)\,, \mathcal{J}_t^0(k,b)\}\,. \tag{4,29}$$

$\mathcal{J}_t^1(\mathcal{J}_t^0)$ represents the optimal discounted expected reward from planning period t until the expiration date T if the option is (not) exercised at time t. Of course, $\mathcal{J}_t$ is the optimal discounted expected reward from period t until T.

Then the optimal decision to exercise the call option at t is defined as follows:

$$f_t(k,b) = \begin{cases} 0 & N(k,b) \leq \mathcal{J}_t^0(k,b) \\ 1 & \text{otherwise}\,. \end{cases} \tag{4,30}$$

If the difference of the posterior expected stock price and the exercise price $N(k,b)$ is not higher than the "option premium" $\mathcal{J}_t^0(k,b)$, then in planning period t it is not optimal to buy stock at the price C.

Because the optimal decision for exercising f_t is a function of the information state (k,b) it will in general not be optimal to make this decision only at the expiration date T. But we will indicate a special case where it is never optimal to exercise before T. To show this we pose the question when a myopic decision rule is optimal for the above mentioned model.

A myopic owner of an option is characterized by a planning horizon of one period. At the beginning of each planning period t, $1 \le t \le T-1$, he is faced with two alternatives: either to exercise the option at t thereby obtaining $N(k,b)$ or to decide buying stock at $t+1$ which results in the amount of $\beta \int q(k,b;\, dr) N(k+1, v(b,r))$. At the expiration date T the owner exercises the option provided that $N(k,b) > 0$ holds.

This leads to the following characterization of the myopic investment policy during the first $T-1$ planning periods:

LEMMA 4.18. *For* $(k,b) \in \mathbf{N} \times \mathbf{R}$ *let*

$$N(k,b) \le \beta \int q(k,b;\, dr) N(k+1, v(b,r))\,. \tag{4,31}$$

Then we have for $1 \le t \le T-1$: $\quad f_t(k,b) = 0$.

PROOF.

$$\begin{aligned} \mathcal{J}_t^0(k,b) &= \beta \int q(k,b;\, dr) \mathcal{J}_{t+1}(k+1, v(b,r)) \\ &\ge \beta \int q(k,b;\, dr) N(k+1, v(b,r)) \\ &\ge N(k,b)\,. \end{aligned}$$

By (4,30) *this just means that we have* $f_t(k,b) = 0$.

The lemma says the following: If the myopic owner who is characterized by (4,31) does not exercise the call option, then the same also holds for the owner who behaves optimally.

Of course, this raises the question when condition (4,31) is valid. We already know from Theorem 2.5 that

$$\int q(k,b;\, dr) N(k+1, v(b,r)) = N(k,b)\,.$$

In this way (4,31) reduces to $N(k,b) \leq \beta N(k,b)$. As the discount factor β is not greater than one, condition (4,31) is satisfied for all information states (k,b) in the case of no discounting, i.e. if $\beta = 1$ holds.

To summarize: In the model without discounting we arrive in the "Black/Scholes–world". The policy for exercising the American call option looks as follows:

$$f_t(k,b) = 0 \quad \text{for all} \quad (k,b) \in \mathbf{N} \times \mathbf{R}, \quad 1 \leq t \leq T-1,$$

$$f_T(k,b) = \begin{cases} 0 & \text{if} \quad N(k,b) \leq 0 \\ 1 & \text{otherwise}. \end{cases}$$

If $\beta = 1$, it is not optimal to exercise the call option before the expiration date T. At T the owner of the option buys stock if the posterior expected stock price exceeds the exercise price C. Otherwise the option expires unexercised and worthless.

But the sensitivity result concerning the discount factor β from Theorem 4.9 shows that the special policy is not optimal in general. There we proved that $\beta_1 < \beta_2$ implies $f_t^1(k,b) \geq f_t^2(k,b)$. Thus, the smaller the discount factor is, the earlier the owner will exercise his American call option.

Other results of our sensitivity analyses are in accordance with the theory of option pricing. There the value of an option, i.e. the option price, increases with the riskiness of the stock as well as with the time to maturity, i.e. the number of periods until the expiration date (cp. e.g. Brealey/Myers (1981), p. 436). Our Theorems 4.10 and 4.13 indicate the same effect but for the option premiums $\mathcal{J}_t^0$.

Like in our model, one assumption in the Black/Scholes model is that the stock does not pay any dividends during the maturation time of the option. If this assumption is violated, it can be advantageous to exercise the American call option before its expiration date.

In our model it is, of course, a challenging task to study the effects of dividend payments on the optimal policy. But this is by far beyond the scope of this chapter, and therefore is devoted to future investigations.

5. Concluding Remarks

The objective of this work was the analysis of dynamic decision models under conditions of uncertainty in the area of investment and portfolio theory. General approaches in this field often did not go beyond the formulation of the model and the statement of the value functions of dynamic programming. Therefore, in most parts of the work we concentrated on models with only two actions; we concentrated on so–called binary models.

In this framework it was possible to derive structural properties of the optimal investment decisions in a qualitative sense. These properties are mainly monotonicity results. In this way the structure of the decision functions turned out to be rather simple and therefore lead to various consequences. First, the optimal investment policy enabled plausible economic interpretations. Furthermore, we succeeded in computing the optimal decisions numerically or at least in finding a starting point for simulation studies. And finally, in this way we are able to obtain many interesting sensitivity results.

By doing so we want to add additional economic structure. Nevertheless we want to maintain the essential structural properties. For example, in the context of the binary portfolio model under conditions of uncertainty this could be the inclusion of transaction costs for switching from one asset to the other. In the dynamic model for the determination of the optimal exercise date of an American call option the consideration of dividend yields during the maturation period of the option is of considerable interest.

To summarize: Structured dynamic programming seems to be a promising tool for the analysis of dynamic economic decision models under conditions of uncertainty.

References

ARROW, Kenneth J. (1971), "Essays in the Theory of Risk Bearing," North-Holland, Amsterdam.

BALDWIN, Carliss Y. (1982), *Optimal Sequential Investment when Capital is not Readily Reversible*, Journal of Finance **37**, 763–782.

BALDWIN, Carliss Y. and Richard F. MEYER (1979), *Liquidity Preference under Uncertainty: A Model of Dynamic Investment in Illiquid Opportunities*, Journal of Financial Economics **7**, 347–374.

BAMBERG, Günter und Adolf Gerhard COENENBERG (1985), "Betriebswirtschaftliche Entscheidungslehre," 4. Aufl., Verlag Vahlen, München.

BARUA, S.K. and G. SRINIVASAN (1987), *Investigation of Decision Criteria for Investment in Risky Assets.*, OMEGA **15**, 247–253.

BENZING, Harald and Michael KOLONKO (1987), *Structured Policies for a Sequential Design Problem with General Distributions*, Mathematics of Operations Research **12**, 60–71.

BENZING, Harald and Werner JAMMERNEGG (1988), *A Bayesian Approach to the Optimal Timing of Investment*, Working Paper, University Graz.

BENZING, Harald and Radu THEODORESCU (1985), *A Sequential Binary Decision Model*, Working Paper, Laval University.

BERGER, James O. (1985), "Statistical Decision Theory and Bayesian Analysis," Second Edition, Springer, New York.

BERNANKE, Ben S. (1983), *Irreversibility, Uncertainty and Cyclical Investment*, Quarterly Journal of Economics **98**, 85–106.

BERNINGHAUS, Siegfried (1985), "Das 'Multi–Armed–Bandit' Paradigma," Athenäum/Hain/Hanstein, Meisenheim.

BERRY, Donald A. and Bert FRISTEDT (1985), "Bandit Problems," Chapman and Hall, London.

BERTSEKAS, Dimitri P. (1974), *Necessary and Sufficient Conditions for Existence of an Optimal Portfolio*, Journal of Economic Theory **8**, 235–247.

BERTSEKAS, Dimitri P. (1976), "Dynamic Programming and Stochastic Control," Academic Press, New York.

BERTSEKAS, Dimitri P. and Steven E. SHREVE (1978), "Stochastic Optimal Control: The Discrete Time Case," Academic Press, New York.

BLACK, Fischer and Myron SCHOLES (1973), *The Pricing of Options and Corporate Liabilities*, Journal of Political Economy **81**, 637–654.

BODILY, Samuel E. and Chelsea C. WHITE (1982), *Optimal Consumption and Portfolio Strategies in a Discrete-Time Model with Summary-Dependent Preferences*, Journal of Financial and Quantitative Analysis **17**, 1–14.

BREALEY, Richard R. and Stewart C. MYERS (1981), "Principles of Corporate Finance," McGraw–Hill, New York.

BRUMELLE, S.L. and R.G. VICKSON (1975), *A Unified Approach to Stochastic Dominance*, in "Stochastic Optimization Models in Finance," Ziemba, W.T. and R.G. Vickson (Eds.), Academic Press, New York, pp. 101–113.

CHEN, Son–Nan and William T. MOORE (1982), *Investment Decisions under Uncertainty: Application of Estimation Risk in the Hillier Approach*, Journal of Financial and Quantitative Analysis **17**, 425–440.

CONSTANTINIDES, George M. (1979), *Multiperiod Consumption and Investment Behavior with Convex Transaction Costs*, Management Science **25**, 1127–1137.

COPELAND, Thomas E. and J. Fred WESTON (1983), "Financial Theory and Corporate Policy," Second Edition, Addison–Wesley, Reading.

CUKIERMAN, Alex (1980), *The Effects of Uncertainty on Investment under Risk Neutrality with Endogenous Information*, Journal of Political Economy **88**, 462–475.

CYERT, Richard M. and Morris H. DE GROOT (1987), "Bayesian Analysis and Uncertainty in Economic Theory," Rowman and Littlefield, Totowa.

DE GROOT, Morris H. (1970), "Optimal Statistical Decisions," McGraw–Hill, New York.

DHINGRA, Harbans L. (1983), *Estimation Risk and Stability of Optimal Portfolio Composition*, European Journal of Operational Research **13**, 353–360.

EATON, Morris L. (1982), *A Review of Selected Topics in Multivariate Probability Inequalities*, Annals of Statistics **10**, 11–43.

ELSTER, K.-H., R. REINHARDT, M. SCHÄUBLE und G. DONATH (1977), "Einführung in die nichtlineare Optimierung," Teubner, Leipzig.

ELTON, Edwin J. and Martin J. GRUBER (1979), *Cash Management*, in "Handbook of Financial Economics," Bicksler, James L. (Ed.), North–Holland, Amsterdam, pp. 205–228.

FAHRMEIR, Ludwig, Heinz KAUFMANN und Friedemann OST (1981), "Stochastische Prozesse," Carl Hanser, München.

FAMA, Eugene F. (1970), *Multiperiod Consumption–Investment Decisions*, American Economic Review **60**, 163–174.

FAMA, Eugene F. (1976), "Foundations of Finance," Basic Books, New York.

FIRCHAU, Volker (1986), "Information Evaluation in Capital Markets," Springer, Berlin.

HAKANSSON, Nils H. (1970), *Optimal Investment and Consumption Strategies under Risk for a Class of Utility Functions*, Econometrica **38**, 587–607.

HAKANSSON, Nils H. (1971), *On Optimal Myopic Portfolio Policies, with and without Serial Correlation of Yields*, Journal of Business **44**, 324–334.

HAKANSSON, Nils H. (1979), *A Characterization of Optimal Multiperiod Portfolio Policies*, TIMS Studies in the Management Sciences **11**, 169–177.

HALEY, Charles W. and Lawrence D. SCHALL (1979), "The Theory of Financial Decisions," Second Edition, McGraw–Hill, New York.

HEANEY, W. John and Robert A. JONES (1988), "The Timing of Investment," Working Paper, Simon Fraser University, Vancouver.

HENGARTNER, Walter, Dieter KALIN and Radu THEODORESCU (1981), *On the Bernoulli Two–Armed Bandit Problem*, Math. Operationsforschung und Statistik, Serie Optimization **12**, 307–316.

HEYMAN, Daniel P. and Matthew J. SOBEL (1984), "Stochastic Models in Operations Research, Volume II," McGraw–Hill, New York.

HINDERER, Karl (1970), "Foundations of Non–stationary Dynamic Programming with Discrete Time Parameter," Springer, Berlin.

HOGG, R.V., D.M. FISHER and R.H. RANDLES (1975), *A Two Sample Adaptive Distribution–Free Test*, Journal of the American Statistical Association **70**, 656–661.

JAMMERNEGG, Werner (1982), *Conditions for Optimality of Isotone Policies in Production–Inventory–Systems*, in "Optimal Control Theory and Economic Analysis," Feichtinger, Gustav (Ed.), North-Holland, Amsterdam, pp. 321–336.

JAMMERNEGG, Werner (1985), *A Dynamic Portfolio Model under Uncertainty: The Two-Point Distribution Case*, in "Optimal Control Theory and Economic Analysis 2," Feichtinger, Gustav (Ed.), North-Holland, Amsterdam, pp. 169–179.

JENNINGS, Robert H. and Christopher B. BARRY (1983), *Information Dissemination and Portfolio Choice*, Journal of Financial and Quantitative Analysis **18**, 1–19.

JOHNSON, Norman L. and Samuel KOTZ (1970), "Distributions in Statistics: Continuous Univariate Distributions 2," John Wiley and Sons, New York.

JONES, Robert A. and Joseph M. OSTROY (1981), *Flexibility and Uncertainty*, Review of Economic Studies **51**, 13–32.

KALLBERG, Jerry G. and William T. ZIEMBA (1984), *Mis- Specifications in Portfolio Selection Problems*, in "Risk and Capital," Bamberg, Günter and Klaus Spremann (Eds.), Springer, Berlin, pp. 74–87.

KANE, Alex (1982), *Skewness Preference and Portfolio Choice*, Journal of Financial and Quantitative Analysis **17**, 15–25.

KISCHKA, Peter (1984), "Bestimmung optimaler Portfolios bei Ungewißheit," Athenäum/Hain/Hanstein, Meisenheim.

KOLONKO, Michael and Harald BENZING (1985), *The Sequential Design of Bernoulli Experiments Including Switching Cost*, Operations Research **33**, 412–426.

LEHMANN, E.L. (1983), "Theory of Point Estimation," John Wiley and Sons, New York.

LINDLEY, D.V. (1970), "Introduction to Probability and Statistics from a Bayesian Viewpoint Part 2. Inference," Cambridge University Press.

LIPPMAN, Steven A. and John J. McCALL (1981), *The Economics of Uncertainty: Selected Topics and Probabilistic Methods*, in "Handbook of Mathematical Economics, Vol. I," Arrow, K.J. and M.D. Intriligator (Eds.), North-Holland, Amsterdam, pp. 211–284.

MAJD, Saman and Robert S. PINDYCK (1987), *Time to Build, Option Value and Investment Decisions*, Journal of Financial Economics **18**, 7–27.

MALLIARIS, A.G. and W.A. BROCK (1982), "Stochastic Methods in Economics and Finance," North-Holland, Amsterdam.

MARGLIN, Stephen A. (1967), "Approaches to Dynamic Investment Planning, Second Printing," North-Holland, Amsterdam.

McDONALD, Robert and Daniel SIEGEL (1986), *The Value of Waiting to Invest*, Quarterly Journal of Economics **101**, 707–727.

McENTIRE, Paul L. (1984), *Portfolio Theory for Independent Assets*, Management Science **30**, 952–963.

MERTON, Robert C. (1982), *On the Microeconomic Theory of Investment under Uncertainty*, in "Handbook of Mathematical Economics, Vol. II," Arrow, K.J. and M.D. Intriligator (Eds.), North–Holland, Amsterdam, pp. 601–669.

MEYER, Jack (1987), *Two-Moment Decision Models and Expected Utility Maximization.*, American Economic Review **77**, 421–430.

MILGROM, Paul R. (1981), *Good News and Bad News: Representation Theorems and Applications*, Bell Journal of Economics **12**, 380–391.

MILLER, Bruce L. (1978), *Optimal Portfolios where Proceeds are a Function of the Current Asset Price*, in "Optimization Techniques Part 2," Stoer, J. (Ed.), Springer, Berlin, pp. 434–442.

MOENE, Karl O. (1985), *Shopping for an Investment Good*, International Economic Review **26**, 351–363.

MOSSIN, Jan (1968), *Optimal Multiperiod Portfolio Policies*, Journal of Business **41**, 215–229.

OLDFIELD, G., R. ROGALSKI and R. JARROW (1977), *An Autoregressive Jump Process for Common Stock Returns*, Journal of Financial Economics **5**, 389–418.

PATEL, J., C.H. KAPADIA and D.B. OWEN (1976), "Handbook of Statistical Distributions," Marcel Dekker, New York.

PERRY, Philip R. (1983), *More Evidence on the Nature of the Distribution of Security Returns*, Journal of Financial and Quantitative Analysis **18**, 211–221.

PHILIPPATOS, George C. (1979), *Mean–Variance Portfolio Selection Strategies*, in "Handbook of Financial Economics," Bicksler, James L. (Ed.), North–Holland, Amsterdam, pp. 309–337.

PRASTACOS, Gregory P. (1983), *Optimal Sequential Investment Decisions under Conditions of Uncertainty*, Management Science **29**, 118–134.

PRATT, John W. (1964), *Risk Aversion in the Small and in the Large*, Econometrica **32**, 122–136.

RIEDER, Ulrich (1975a), *Bayesian Dynamic Programming*, Advances in Applied Probability **7**, 330–348.

RIEDER, Ulrich (1975b), *On Stopped Decision Processes with Discrete Time Parameter*, Stochastic Processes and their Applications **3**, 365–383.

ROBERTS, Kevin and Martin L. WEITZMAN (1981), *Funding Criteria for Research, Development, and Exploration Projects*, Econometrica **49**, 1261–1288.

ROHATGI, V.K. (1976), "An Introduction to Probability Theory and Mathematical Statistics," John Wiley and Sons, New York.

ROTHSCHILD, Michael and Joseph E. STIGLITZ (1970), *Increasing Risk: I. A Definition*, Journal of Economic Theory **2**, 225–243.

SAMUELSON, Paul A. (1969), *Lifetime Portfolio Selection by Dynamic Stochastic Programming*, The Review of Economics and Statistics **51**, 239–246.

SERFOZO, Richard F. (1976), *Monotone Optimal Policies for Markov Decision Processes*, Mathematical Programming Study **6**, 202–215.

SIMKOWITZ, Michael A. and William L. BEEDLES (1978), *Diversification in a Three-Moment World*, Journal of Financial and Quantitative Analysis **13**, 927–941.

STOYAN, Dietrich (1983), "Comparison Methods for Queues and Other Stochastic Models," John Wiley and Sons, New York.

SWOBODA, Peter (1977), "Investition und Finanzierung," 2. Auflage, Vandenhoeck und Ruprecht, Göttingen.

SWOBODA, Peter (1981), "Betriebliche Finanzierung," Physica, Würzburg.

TESFATSION, Leigh (1981), *Dynamic Investment, Risk Aversion and Foresight Sensitivity*, Journal of Economic Dynamics and Control **3**, 65–96.

UHLIR, Helmut und Peter STEINER (1986), "Wertpapieranalyse," Physica, Heidelberg.

VENEZIA, Itzhak (1983), *A Bayesian Approach to the Optimal Growth Period Problem*, Journal of Finance **38**, 237–246.

WILHELM, Jochen (1983), *Marktwertmaximierung - Ein didaktisch einfacher Zugang zu einem Grundlagenproblem der Investitions- und Finanzierungstheorie*, Zeitschrift für Betriebswirtschaft **53**, 516–534.

WINKLER, Robert L. (1973), *Bayesian Models for Forecasting Future Security Prices*, Journal of Financial and Quantitative Analysis **8**, 387–405.

WINKLER, Robert L. (1979), *Statistical Decision Theory and Financial Decision-Making*, in "Handbook of Financial Economics," Bicksler, James L. (Ed.), North–Holland, Amsterdam, pp. 395–413.

WINKLER, Robert L. and Christopher B. BARRY (1975), *A Bayesian Model for Portfolio Selection and Revision*, Journal of Finance **30**, 179–192.

Subject Index

Vol. 211: P. van den Heuvel, The Stability of a Macroeconomic System with Quantity Constraints. VII, 169 pages. 1983.

Vol. 212: R. Sato and T. Nôno, Invariance Principles and the Structure of Technology. V, 94 pages. 1983.

Vol. 213: Aspiration Levels in Bargaining and Economic Decision Making. Proceedings, 1982. Edited by R. Tietz. VIII, 406 pages. 1983.

Vol. 214: M. Faber, H. Niemes und G. Stephan, Entropie, Umweltschutz und Rohstoffverbrauch. IX, 181 Seiten. 1983.

Vol. 215: Semi-Infinite Programming and Applications. Proceedings, 1981. Edited by A.V. Fiacco and K.O. Kortanek. XI, 322 pages. 1983.

Vol. 216: H.H. Müller, Fiscal Policies in a General Equilibrium Model with Persistent Unemployment. VI, 92 pages. 1983.

Vol. 217: Ch. Grootaert, The Relation Between Final Demand and Income Distribution. XIV, 105 pages. 1983.

Vol. 218: P. van Loon, A Dynamic Theory of the Firm: Production, Finance and Investment. VII, 191 pages. 1983.

Vol. 219: E. van Damme, Refinements of the Nash Equilibrium Concept. VI, 151 pages. 1983.

Vol. 220: M. Aoki, Notes on Economic Time Series Analysis: System Theoretic Perspectives. IX, 249 pages. 1983.

Vol. 221: S. Nakamura, An Inter-Industry Translog Model of Prices and Technical Change for the West German Economy. XIV, 290 pages. 1984.

Vol. 222: P. Meier, Energy Systems Analysis for Developing Countries. VI, 344 pages. 1984.

Vol. 223: W. Trockel, Market Demand. VIII, 205 pages. 1984.

Vol. 224: M. Kiy, Ein disaggregiertes Prognosesystem für die Bundesrepublik Deutschland. XVIII, 276 Seiten. 1984.

Vol. 225: T.R. von Ungern-Sternberg, Zur Analyse von Märkten mit unvollständiger Nachfragerinformation. IX, 125 Seiten. 1984

Vol. 226: Selected Topics in Operations Research and Mathematical Economics. Proceedings, 1983. Edited by G. Hammer and D. Pallaschke. IX, 478 pages. 1984.

Vol. 227: Risk and Capital. Proceedings, 1983. Edited by G. Bamberg and K. Spremann. VII, 306 pages. 1984.

Vol. 228: Nonlinear Models of Fluctuating Growth. Proceedings, 1983. Edited by R.M. Goodwin, M. Krüger and A. Vercelli. XVII, 277 pages. 1984.

Vol. 229: Interactive Decision Analysis. Proceedings, 1983. Edited by M. Grauer and A.P. Wierzbicki. VIII, 269 pages. 1984.

Vol. 230: Macro-Economic Planning with Conflicting Goals. Proceedings, 1982. Edited by M. Despontin, P. Nijkamp and J. Spronk. VI, 297 pages. 1984.

Vol. 231: G.F. Newell, The M/M/∞ Service System with Ranked Servers in Heavy Traffic. XI, 126 pages. 1984.

Vol. 232: L. Bauwens, Bayesian Full Information Analysis of Simultaneous Equation Models Using Integration by Monte Carlo. VI, 114 pages. 1984.

Vol. 233: G. Wagenhals, The World Copper Market. XI, 190 pages. 1984.

Vol. 234: B.C. Eaves, A Course in Triangulations for Solving Equations with Deformations. III, 302 pages. 1984.

Vol. 235: Stochastic Models in Reliability Theory. Proceedings, 1984. Edited by S. Osaki and Y. Hatoyama. VII, 212 pages. 1984.

Vol. 236: G. Gandolfo, P.C. Padoan, A Disequilibrium Model of Real and Financial Accumulation in an Open Economy. VI, 172 pages. 1984.

Vol. 237: Misspecification Analysis. Proceedings, 1983. Edited by T.K. Dijkstra. V, 129 pages. 1984.

Vol. 238: W. Domschke, A. Drexl, Location and Layout Planning. IV, 134 pages. 1985.

Vol. 239: Microeconomic Models of Housing Markets. Edited by K. Stahl. VII, 197 pages. 1985.

Vol. 240: Contributions to Operations Research. Proceedings, 1984. Edited by K. Neumann and D. Pallaschke. V, 190 pages. 1985.

Vol. 241: U. Wittmann, Das Konzept rationaler Preiserwartungen. XI, 310 Seiten. 1985.

Vol. 242: Decision Making with Multiple Objectives. Proceedings, 1984. Edited by Y.Y. Haimes and V. Chankong. XI, 571 pages. 1985.

Vol. 243: Integer Programming and Related Areas. A Classified Bibliography 1981–1984. Edited by R. von Randow. XX, 386 pages. 1985.

Vol. 244: Advances in Equilibrium Theory. Proceedings, 1984. Edited by C.D. Aliprantis, O. Burkinshaw and N.J. Rothman. II, 235 pages. 1985.

Vol. 245: J.E.M. Wilhelm, Arbitrage Theory. VII, 114 pages. 1985.

Vol. 246: P.W. Otter, Dynamic Feature Space Modelling, Filtering and Self-Tuning Control of Stochastic Systems. XIV, 177 pages. 1985.

Vol. 247: Optimization and Discrete Choice in Urban Systems. Proceedings, 1983. Edited by B.G. Hutchinson, P. Nijkamp and M. Batty. VI, 371 pages. 1985.

Vol. 248: Plural Rationality and Interactive Decision Processes. Proceedings, 1984. Edited by M. Grauer, M. Thompson and A.P. Wierzbicki. VI, 354 pages. 1985.

Vol. 249: Spatial Price Equilibrium: Advances in Theory, Computation and Application. Proceedings, 1984. Edited by P. T. Harker. VII, 277 pages. 1985.

Vol. 250: M. Roubens, Ph. Vincke, Preference Modelling. VIII, 94 pages. 1985.

Vol. 251: Input-Output Modeling. Proceedings, 1984. Edited by A. Smyshlyaev. VI, 261 pages. 1985.

Vol. 252: A. Birolini, On the Use of Stochastic Processes in Modeling Reliability Problems. VI, 105 pages. 1985.

Vol. 253: C. Withagen, Economic Theory and International Trade in Natural Exhaustible Resources. VI, 172 pages. 1985.

Vol. 254: S. Müller, Arbitrage Pricing of Contingent Claims. VIII, 151 pages. 1985.

Vol. 255: Nondifferentiable Optimization: Motivations and Applications. Proceedings, 1984. Edited by V.F. Demyanov and D. Pallaschke. VI, 350 pages. 1985.

Vol. 256: Convexity and Duality in Optimization. Proceedings, 1984. Edited by J. Ponstein. V, 142 pages. 1985.

Vol. 257: Dynamics of Macrosystems. Proceedings, 1984. Edited by J.-P. Aubin, D. Saari and K. Sigmund. VI, 280 pages. 1985.

Vol. 258: H. Funke, Eine allgemeine Theorie der Polypol- und Oligopolpreisbildung. III, 237 pages. 1985.

Vol. 259: Infinite Programming. Proceedings, 1984. Edited by E.J. Anderson and A.B. Philpott. XIV, 244 pages. 1985.

Vol. 260: H.-J. Kruse, Degeneracy Graphs and the Neighbourhood Problem. VIII, 128 pages. 1986.

Vol. 261: Th.R. Gulledge, Jr., N.K. Womer, The Economics of Made-to-Order Production. VI, 134 pages. 1986.

Vol. 262: H.U. Buhl, A Neo-Classical Theory of Distribution and Wealth. V, 146 pages. 1986.

Vol. 263: M. Schäfer, Resource Extraction and Market Structure. XI, 154 pages. 1986.

Vol. 264: Models of Economic Dynamics. Proceedings, 1983. Edited by H.F. Sonnenschein. VII, 212 pages. 1986.

Vol. 265: Dynamic Games and Applications in Economics. Edited by T. Başar. IX, 288 pages. 1986.

Vol. 266: Multi-Stage Production Planning and Inventory Control. Edited by S. Axsäter, Ch. Schneeweiss and E. Silver. V, 264 pages. 1986.

Vol. 267: R. Bemelmans, The Capacity Aspect of Inventories. IX, 165 pages. 1986.

Vol. 268: V. Firchau, Information Evaluation in Capital Markets. VII, 103 pages. 1986.

Vol. 269: A. Borglin, H. Keiding, Optimality in Infinite Horizon Economies. VI, 180 pages. 1986.

Vol. 270: Technological Change, Employment and Spatial Dynamics. Proceedings 1985. Edited by P. Nijkamp. VII, 466 pages. 1986.

Vol. 271: C. Hildreth, The Cowles Commission in Chicago, 1939–1955. V, 176 pages. 1986.

Vol. 272: G. Clemenz, Credit Markets with Asymmetric Information. VIII, 212 pages. 1986.

Vol. 273: Large-Scale Modelling and Interactive Decision Analysis. Proceedings, 1985. Edited by G. Fandel, M. Grauer, A. Kurzhanski and A.P. Wierzbicki. VII, 363 pages. 1986.

Vol. 274: W.K. Klein Haneveld, Duality in Stochastic Linear and Dynamic Programming. VII, 295 pages. 1986.

Vol. 275: Competition, Instability, and Nonlinear Cycles. Proceedings, 1985. Edited by W. Semmler. XII, 340 pages. 1986.

Vol. 276: M.R. Baye, D.A. Black, Consumer Behavior, Cost of Living Measures, and the Income Tax. VII, 119 pages. 1986.

Vol. 277: Studies in Austrian Capital Theory, Investment and Time. Edited by M. Faber. VI, 317 pages. 1986.

Vol. 278: W.E. Diewert, The Measurement of the Economic Benefits of Infrastructure Services. V, 202 pages. 1986.

Vol. 279: H.-J. Büttler, G. Frei and B. Schips, Estimation of Disequilibrium Models. VI, 114 pages. 1986.

Vol. 280: H.T. Lau, Combinatorial Heuristic Algorithms with FORTRAN. VII, 126 pages. 1986.

Vol. 281: Ch.-L. Hwang, M.-J. Lin, Group Decision Making under Multiple Criteria. XI, 400 pages. 1987.

Vol. 282: K. Schittkowski, More Test Examples for Nonlinear Programming Codes. V, 261 pages. 1987.

Vol. 283: G. Gabisch, H.-W. Lorenz, Business Cycle Theory. VII, 229 pages. 1987.

Vol. 284: H. Lütkepohl, Forecasting Aggregated Vector ARMA Processes. X, 323 pages. 1987.

Vol. 285: Toward Interactive and Intelligent Decision Support Systems. Volume 1. Proceedings, 1986. Edited by Y. Sawaragi, K. Inoue and H. Nakayama. XII, 445 pages. 1987.

Vol. 286: Toward Interactive and Intelligent Decision Support Systems. Volume 2. Proceedings, 1986. Edited by Y. Sawaragi, K. Inoue and H. Nakayama. XII, 450 pages. 1987.

Vol. 287: Dynamical Systems. Proceedings, 1985. Edited by A.B. Kurzhanski and K. Sigmund. VI, 215 pages. 1987.

Vol. 288: G.D. Rudebusch, The Estimation of Macroeconomic Disequilibrium Models with Regime Classification Information. VII, 128 pages. 1987.

Vol. 289: B.R. Meijboom, Planning in Decentralized Firms. X, 168 pages. 1987.

Vol. 290: D.A. Carlson, A. Haurie, Infinite Horizon Optimal Control. XI, 254 pages. 1987.

Vol. 291: N. Takahashi, Design of Adaptive Organizations. VI, 140 pages. 1987.

Vol. 292: I. Tchijov, L. Tomaszewicz (Eds.), Input-Output Modeling. Proceedings, 1985. VI, 195 pages. 1987.

Vol. 293: D. Batten, J. Casti, B. Johansson (Eds.), Economic Evolution and Structural Adjustment. Proceedings, 1985. VI, 382 pages. 1987.

Vol. 294: J. Jahn, W. Krabs (Eds.), Recent Advances and Historical Development of Vector Optimization. VII, 405 pages. 1987.

Vol. 295: H. Meister, The Purification Problem for Constrained Games with Incomplete Information. X, 127 pages. 1987.

Vol. 296: A. Börsch-Supan, Econometric Analysis of Discrete Choice. VIII, 211 pages. 1987.

Vol. 297: V. Fedorov, H. Läuter (Eds.), Model-Oriented Data Analysis. Proceedings, 1987. VI, 239 pages. 1988.

Vol. 298: S.H. Chew, Q. Zheng, Integral Global Optimization. VII, 179 pages. 1988.

Vol. 299: K. Marti, Descent Directions and Efficient Solutions in Discretely Distributed Stochastic Programs. XIV, 178 pages. 1988.

Vol. 300: U. Derigs, Programming in Networks and Graphs. XI, 315 pages. 1988.

Vol. 301: J. Kacprzyk, M. Roubens (Eds.), Non-Conventional Preference Relations in Decision Making. VII, 155 pages. 1988.

Vol. 302: H.A. Eiselt, G. Pederzoli (Eds.), Advances in Optimization and Control. Proceedings, 1986. VIII, 372 pages. 1988.

Vol. 303: F.X. Diebold, Empirical Modeling of Exchange Rate Dynamics. VII, 143 pages. 1988.

Vol. 304: A. Kurzhanski, K. Neumann, D. Pallaschke (Eds.), Optimization, Parallel Processing and Applications. Proceedings, 1987. VI, 292 pages. 1988.

Vol. 305: G.-J.C.Th. van Schijndel, Dynamic Firm and Investor Behaviour under Progressive Personal Taxation. X, 215 pages. 1988.

Vol. 306: Ch. Klein, A Static Microeconomic Model of Pure Competition. VIII, 139 pages. 1988.

Vol. 307: T.K. Dijkstra (Ed.), On Model Uncertainty and its Statistical Implications. VII, 138 pages. 1988.

Vol. 308: J.R. Daduna, A. Wren (Eds.), Computer-Aided Transit Scheduling. VIII, 339 pages. 1988.

Vol. 309: G. Ricci, K. Velupillai (Eds.), Growth Cycle and Multisectoral Economics: the Goodwin Tradition. III, 126 pages. 1988.

Vol. 310: J. Kacprzyk, M. Fedrizzi (Eds.), Combining Fuzzy Imprecision with Probabilistic Uncertainty in Decision Making. IX, 399 pages. 1988.

Vol. 311: R. Färe, Fundamentals of Production Theory. IX, 163 pages. 1988.

Vol. 312: J. Krishnakumar, Estimation of Simultaneous Equation Models with Error Components Structure. X, 357 pages. 1988.

Vol. 313: W. Jammernegg, Sequential Binary Investment Decisions. VI, 156 pages. 1988.

GPSR Compliance

The European Union's (EU) General Product Safety Regulation (GPSR) is a set of rules that requires consumer products to be safe and our obligations to ensure this.

If you have any concerns about our products, you can contact us on ProductSafety@springernature.com

In case Publisher is established outside the EU, the EU authorized representative is:

Springer Nature Customer Service Center GmbH
Europaplatz 3
69115 Heidelberg, Germany

Batch number: 10838062

Printed by Printforce, the Netherlands